Northumberland & the Scottish Borders

Walks

Compiled by
Dennis and Jan Kelsall

GW00367749

Text: Dennis and Jan Kelsall
Photography: Brian Conduit, Dennis and Jan Kelsall
Editorial: Ark Creative (UK) Ltd
Design: Ark Creative (UK) Ltd

This product includes mapping data licensed from Ordnance Survey® with the permission of the Controller of Her Majesty's Stationery Office. © Crown Copyright 2010. All rights reserved. Licence number 150002047. Ordnance Survey, the OS symbol and Pathfinder are registered trademarks and Explorer, Landranger and Outdoor Leisure are trademarks of the Ordnance Survey, the national mapping agency of Great Britain.

ISBN: 978-1-85458-551-6

While every care has been taken to ensure the accuracy of the route directions, the publishers cannot accept responsibility for errors or omissions, or for changes in details given. The countryside is not static: hedges and fences can be removed, field boundaries can alter, footpaths can be rerouted and changes in ownership can result in the closure or diversion of some concessionary paths. Also, paths that are easy and pleasant for walking in fine conditions may become slippery, muddy and difficult in wet weather, while stepping stones across rivers and streams may become impassable.

If you find an inaccuracy in either the text or maps, please write to Crimson Publishing at the address below.

First published 2003 by Jarrold Publishing

First published in Great Britain 2010 by Crimson Publishing, a division of:
Crimson Business Ltd,
Westminster House, Kew Road, Richmond, Surrey, TW9 2ND

www.totalwalking.co.uk

Printed in Singapore. 12/10

Front cover: Hadrian's Wall from Peel Crags
Previous page: Dunstanburgh Castle is a famous Northumberland landmark

Contents

Approximate walk times

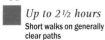 Up to 2½ hours
Short walks on generally clear paths

 2½–3½ hours
Slightly harder walks of moderate length

 3½ hours and over
Longer walks including some steep ascents/descents, occasionally on faint paths

The walk times are provided as a guide only and are calculated using an average walking speed of 2½mph (4km/h), adding one minute for each 10m (33ft) of ascent, and then rounding the result to the nearest half hour.

Walks are considered to be dog friendly unless specified.

KIRKCALDY
KINGHORN
BURNTISLAND

NORTH BERWICK
Bass Rock
Dirleton
Gullane
EAST LINTON
HADDINGTON
Longniddry
COCKENZIE AND PORT SETON
PRESTONPANS
MUSSELBURGH
EDINBURGH
TRANENT
Gifford

DALKEITH
LOANHEAD
LASSWADE
BONNYRIGG
Mayfield
Newtongrange
PENICUIK
Gorebridge

MOORFOOT HILLS
LAMMERMUIR

LAUDER
Oxton

18 PEEBLES
Kings Muir
INNERLEITHEN
27
Walkerburn
GALASHIELS
24 MELROSE
14
Earlston
St Boswells

SELKIRK
Philiphaugh
Ancrum

A68

HAWICK
Denholm

CRAIK FOREST

SCALE 1:384 615 or 1 INCH to about 6 MILES *1CM to 3.8KM*

0   2   4   6   8   10 KILOMETRES   15

0   2   4   6   MILES 8   10

KEYMAP HEIGHTS SHOWN IN METRES

DUNBAR
Broxburn
Barns Ness
Skateraw
Torness Point
Cement Works
Power Sta
Thorntonloch
Innerwick
Castle
Reed Point
Cocklaw Hill
Cockburnspath
Oldhamstocks
Pease Bay
Siccar Point
Wheat Stack
East Castle
Ecclaw
Fort
St ABB'S HEAD
13
Telegraph Hill
Lumsdaine
St Abbs
Coldingham Bay
Upland Way
Blackburn Rig
Grantshouse
Coldingham Priory
Buss Craig
EYEMOUTH
Abbey St Bathans
9
Houndwood
Burnmouth
Cranshaws
Ellemford
Longformacus
Marygold
Auchencrow
Reston
Ayton
Lamberton Beach
Preston
Linthill
Chirnside
Edrom
Chirnsidebridge
Foulden
Clappers
Lamberton
Choicelee
Whitsome
Allanton
Paxton
BERWICK-UPON-TWEED
Polwarth
Fogo
New Horndean
East Ord
Gavinton
DUNS
Manderston
Blackadder
Fishwick
Screremerston
Cheswick Black Rocks
Greenlaw
A697
Swintonmill
Ladykirk
Norham
Shoreswood
Cheswick
A6105
Leitholm
Upsettlington
Grindon
Felkington
Haggerston
A1
Goswick
12
HOLY ISLAND
Eccles
Orange Lane
Lennel
Duddo
Bowsden
West Mains
Holy Island Sands
Priory
Humehall
Stichill
Birgham
Cornhill on Tweed
Heaton
Barmoor Lane End
East Kyloe
Guile Point
KELSO
19
Carham
Wark
East Learmouth
Pressen
Branxton
Ford
Kimmerston
Lowick
Buckton
Detchant
Elwick
Heiton
Hadden
Mindrum
Downham
Flodden
Fenton
17
Belford
Easington
Spindlestone
Bowmont Forest
Lempitlaw
Pawston
Milfield
Lanton
Ewart Newtown
Doddington
Horton
Warenton
Belsay
Crookhouse
Shotton
Westnewton
Kirknewton
Akeld
Humbleton
3
Chatton
Greendykes
Rosebrough
Town Yetholm
Kirk Yetholm
23
Yeavering Bell
WOOLER
Haugh Head
Chillingham
Newtown
Hepburn
Middle Moor
Brownleside
Morebattle
Linton
Nethpool
Earle
Liburn Tower
East Lilburn
Old Bewick
West Lilburn
Whitton
Howgate
Langleeford
28
THE CHEVIOT
Hedgehope Hill
South Middleton
Langlee Crags
Roddam
Wooperton
West Ditchburn
Swinside
Crask Moor
Southope
Auchope Cairn
Comb Fell
Ilderton
Roseden
New Bewick
Eglingham
Oxnam
Chatto
A697
Ingram
Brandon
Beanley
Shawdon Hall
Bolton
Hartside
Linhope
Shill Moor
25
Prendwick
Branton
Glanton Pyke
Glanton
Powburn
Abberwick
ALN
Windy Gyle
Bloodybush Edge
Cushat Law
High Knowes
Great Ryle
Whittingham
Broome Park
Hulne Park
22
NORTHUMBERLAND NATIONAL PARK
Barrowburn
Warton
Prendwick
Little Ryle
Yelington
Shawdon Wood
Corbridge
Long
Alwinton
Biddlestone
Netherton
Burradon
Scrainwood
Yetlington
Callaly
Thrunton Wood
Castle
Edlingham

Keymap 2

24
14
19
23
4
22
10
1
26
16
8
21
5
GALASHIELS
MELROSE
KELSO
SELKIRK
HAWICK
JEDBURGH
Town Yetholm
Kirk Yetholm
Newcastleton or Copshaw Holm
Bellingham
Haltwhistle
Haydon Bridge
Brampton
Wetheral
Carter Bar
THE CHEVIOTS
WAUCHOPE FOREST
REDESDALE FOREST
KIELDER FOREST
KIELDER WATER
NEWCASTLETON FOREST
KERSHOPE FOREST
WARK FOREST
Spadeadam Forest
LIDDESDALE
Larriston Fells
Kielderhead Moor
Peel Fell
Kielder
Hadrian's Wall Path
Pennine Way
DERE STREET
A7
A68
A698
A699
A6088
A69
A689
A686
A6071
B6357
B6318
B6320
M6

SCALE 1:384 615 or 1 INCH to about 6 MILES *1CM to 3.8KM*

0 2 4 6 8 10 KILOMETRES 15

0 2 4 MILES 8 10

KEYMAP HEIGHTS SHOWN IN METRES

At-a-glance

Walk	Page	Start	Nat. Grid Reference	Distance	Time	Height Gain
Allen Banks	22	Allen Banks	NY 798639	3½ miles (5.6km)	2 hrs	770ft (235m)
Arnton Fell	32	Arnton Fell	NY 514932	5 miles (8km)	2½ hrs	1,115ft (340m)
Blanchland	16	Blanchland	NY 964504	3½ miles (5.6km)	2 hrs	525ft (160m)
Bolam Lake and Shaftoe Crags	45	Bolam Lake Country Park	NZ 083820	6½ miles (10.5km)	3 hrs	540ft (165m)
Cauldshiels Loch and the River Tweed	73	Gun Knowe Loch, Tweedbank	NT 517346	10 miles (16.1km)	4½ hrs	1,150ft (350m)
The Cheviot from Harthope Valley	88	Hawsen Bridge, Harthope Valley	NT 953225	13¼ miles (21.3km)	7 hrs	3,280ft (1,000m)
Coldingham Bay and St Abb's Head	40	Coldingham Bay	NT 915665	5¾ miles (9.3km)	3 hrs	1,015ft (310m)
Craster and Dunstanburgh Castle	24	Craster	NU 256198	4¾ miles (7.6km)	2 hrs	380ft (115m)
Craster, Howick and Longhoughton	60	Craster	NU 256198	8 miles (12.9km)	3½ hrs	605ft (185m)
Doddington Moor	18	Doddington	NT 999323	4 miles (6.4km)	2 hrs	540ft (165m)
Hadrian's Wall, Housesteads, Sewingshields Crags	80	Housesteads	NY 793684	9 miles (14.5km)	4½ hrs	1,180ft (360m)
Hadrian's Wall from Once Brewed	48	Once Brewed	NY 752668	6¾ miles (10.9km)	3 hrs	900ft (275m)
Hadrian's Wall from Steel Rigg	28	Steel Rigg	NY 751676	4¾ miles (7.6km)	2½ hrs	770ft (235m)
Hadrian's Wall at Walltown and Thirlwall Castle	63	Walltown Quarry	NY 668659	7¾ miles (12.5km)	3½ hrs	1,020ft (310m)
Hartside, Salter's Road and High Cantle	76	Hartside	NT 976161	8½ miles (13.7km)	4½ hrs	1,590ft (485m)
Kelso, Roxburgh and the River Teviot	57	Kelso	NT 727339	7½ miles (12.1km)	3½ hrs	510ft (155m)
Kielder Water – the Bull Crag Peninsula	14	Bull Crag Peninsula	NY 677870	3 miles (4.8km)	1½ hrs	280ft (85m)
Kirk Yetholm and the Halterburn Valley	70	Kirk Yetholm	NT 827281	8½ miles (13.6km)	4½ hrs	2,115ft (645m)
Lindisfarne	37	Holy Island	NU 125425	5½ miles (8.8km)	2½ hrs	195ft (60m)
Melrose and the Eildon Hills	42	Melrose	NT 547339	5 miles (8km)	3 hrs	1,475ft (450m)
Peebles and the River Tweed	54	Peebles	NT 249403	7¼ miles (11.7km)	3 hrs	560ft (170m)
Peniel Heugh	20	Harestanes	NT 641244	4½ miles (7.2km)	2 hrs	625ft (190m)
Above Rothbury	34	Rothbury	NU 050015	5¼ miles (8.5km)	2½ hrs	820ft (250m)
Simonside	26	Simonside Forest Park	NZ 036996	4½ miles (7.2km)	2½ hrs	920ft (280m)
St Cuthbert's Cave	51	Holburn Grange	NU 051351	7 miles (11.3km)	3½ hrs	785ft (240m)
Traquair and Minch Moor	84	Innerleithen	NT 335357	9¾ miles (15.7km)	5 hrs	1,820ft (555m)
Whiteadder Valley and Edin's Hall Broch	30	Abbey St Bathans	NT 762618	5 miles (8km)	2½ hrs	870ft (265m)
Windy Gyle	67	Rowhope Burn Bridge	NT 859114	7¼ miles (11.7km)	4 hrs	1,640ft (500m)

Comments

Created during the middle decades of the 19th century, the charming woodland gardens at Allen Banks line a narrow gorge containing the river. This exploration takes in The Tarn.

Overlooking Hermitage Castle on the edge of the 'Disputed Lands', Arnton Fell offers an enjoyable hill walk and stunning views in an area often ignored by ramblers.

Famed as one of England's prettiest villages, Blanchland is the start point for this enjoyable, short walk through woodland onto the edge of the moor.

Set apart from the main range of Northumberland hills, Shaftoe Crags are an impressive sandstone outcrop. Their name remembers the Shafto family.

Sir Walter Scott's home, a delightful local beauty spot and a grand walk beside the River Tweed are combined in this ramble from a small loch on the edge of Galashiels.

The Cheviot is the highest mountain in Northumberland. In fine weather, this approach makes a grand day out, but as the steepest gradients come later on, *it is for fit and experienced walkers only.*

The cliff scenery at St Abb's Head is among the most dramatic on the east coast, seen on this walk beginning from the superb sandy cove of Coldingham Bay.

Dunstanburgh Castle is one of the most evocative sights along the Northumberland coast, reached here on a popular walk from the picturesque village of Craster.

The coastline south of Craster is often ignored, but offers a grand walk past several inviting bays. The inland return passes Howick Hall, where the gardens are open early spring to late autumn.

The heather and bracken moors above Doddington conceal many traces of prehistoric settlement, including a stone circle, ring fort and many less obvious carvings on the boulders littering the hill.

At Sewing Shields, Hadrian's Wall begins its most spectacular section along the Great Win Sill, overlooking an untamed landscape that once belonged to the Caledonians.

One of the best-preserved sections of Hadrian's Wall lies to the east of Cawfield Crags. It is explored here on a walk from the National Park information centre.

The walk follows a particularly dramatic section of Hadrian's Wall, returning past a small lough to get a stunning view back to the line of crags along which it runs.

Explore the Roman wall at first hand and then call in at the Greenhead Roman Army Museum to learn about the lives of the men stationed along this distant frontier of the Roman Empire.

The River Breamish has its source in the Cheviot Hills. This roving circuit explores the deserted hills above Hartside and Linhope, and includes an optional diversion to an impressive waterfall.

The ruins of Kelso's abbey are just one of the highlights passed on this walk which begins along an old railway and returns beside the river past the site of old Roxburgh and its castle.

With Britain's most capacious reservoir and Europe's largest planted woodland, Kielder Forest Park is a superb outdoor activity area for everyone as revealed in this undemanding stroll.

The pub at Kirk Yetholm used to provide a free half-pint to walkers completing the Pennine Way courtesy of Alfred Wainwright. This rewarding trek combines the two options for the last leg of the journey.

St Aidan settled on the Holy Island of Lindisfarne when he brought Christianity to Northumbria in the 7th century. The beautiful and tranquil island remains a place of pilgrimage.

The distinctive profile of the Eildon Hills is glimpsed from several of the walks in this collection. They are ascended here from the old town of Melrose, famous for its abbey and walled flower garden.

'Peebles for Pleasure' went the old saying, and there is certainly much of that in this superb wander along the River Tweed from the attractive old border town.

The Waterloo Monument rising above the wooded flanks of Peniel Heugh is a prominent landmark and great viewpoint and is visited here from the craft and visitor centre at Harestanes.

Combine this walk on his moorland estate above Rothbury with a visit to nearby Cragside, Lord Armstrong's innovative country mansion, which is now cared for by the National Trust.

A superb sandstone hill overlooking Coquetdale, its upper crags a favourite of climbers, Simonside makes a grand objective for this enjoyable ramble.

St Cuthbert's Cave is one of many places throughout Northumberland associated with the 7th-century Celtic saint. The line of low hills below which it is tucked give a fine panorama across the countryside.

The highest point on the eastern section of the Southern Upland Way lies across the flank of Minch Moor. It is combined here with a forest ramble and an easy finish along the valley of the River Tweed.

Set above the unspoiled valley of Whiteadder Water, Edin's Hall Broch is one of the finest examples of surviving Iron Age architecture in the region.

Windy Gyle often lives up to its name, but is nevertheless a superb spot along the Pennine Way as it snakes across the Cheviot Hills. The hill is reached here from the lonely valley of Upper Coquetdale.

At-a-glance

Introduction to Northumberland and the Scottish Borders

Introduction

The region covered within this book encompasses a vast swathe of land straddling the border between Scotland and England. It lies within two counties, the Scottish Borders and Northumberland, both coincidentally ranked in terms of area as sixth within their respective countries and having a combined size almost half that of Wales. But, despite the wavering dotted line that snakes across the map, it is sometimes hard to regard it as two separate countries. True, there are places where the distinction might easily be made by listening to the song in the speech of the people around or by looking at the place names on a sign, but even here there are no hard and fast rules. There are many English-looking names well north of the border and, with so many variations of accent and dialect, strangers to the area might justifiably feel they were in a different country altogether.

A troubled region

Indeed, in some ways, their perception is not misplaced, for the disparate sides of today's border have a great deal in common – a shared history of conflict. The Roman scholar Tacitus, in writing his history of the Roman Empire, attributed a speech to the Pictish leader Calgacus before his defeat at the hand of Tacitus' father-in-law Agricola during the battle of Mons Graupis in AD83, in which he said 'solitudinem faciunt, pacem appellant – They make a desert and they call it peace'. His words might well have been applied to the land here, for during the first 1,600 years of recorded history, the Borders have been a troubled region, repeatedly harassed and ravaged by forces from both sides intent upon subjugation or merely plundering their neighbour's goods in anarchical lawlessness. From the days of the Romans to the Union of the Crowns under James in 1603, trouble was never far away and the people often went cold and hungry, their homes burned, their crops destroyed and their cattle stolen.

That history is evident in the defensive walls, castles, peles, bastles and tower houses scattered across the region. Hadrian's Wall is the earliest and perhaps best known of these, started in 122 and cutting right across the country from the Solway Firth to the estuary of the Tyne. The complex defence incorporated several large forts and military roads as well as milecastles and turrets placed at regular intervals along the wall itself. In the period that followed, the area became united under the Anglo-Saxon kingdom of Northumbria, which once stretched from the Humber to the Forth. It grew great as a centre of both secular and religious culture, King Oswald bringing missionaries and scholars from the Celtic religious centre on Iona. But by the end of the first millennium the kingdom had become fragmented, laying the seeds of future territorial dispute. Even that time, however, had not been a period of peace, for Viking raiders from across the North Sea repeatedly pillaged the coastal settlements. Religious communities were particularly vulnerable because of their relative wealth and the monks at Lindisfarne were eventually forced to abandon their island, taking their precious relics with them.

Having subdued the heartland of England, William the Conqueror turned his unwelcome attentions to the North. His onslaught was particularly brutal, massacring whole villages and salting the land to prevent recovery and rebellion. Both sides of the border were left under the rule of the Marcher Lords and for the next 400 years, the passage of English and Scottish armies, battles and reiver raids disrupted life and progress. The border moved back and forth like the ebb and flow of the tide and the town of Berwick changed hands no less than 13 times during this period. The need for security was paramount and apart from strategic castles built by the Scottish and English kings, landowners of any standing raised their own defences, great and small. Even after the unification under James, peace was occasionally an elusive quality, Cromwell's armies wrought destruction on their northern campaigns and Northumbria was generally sympathetic to the Jacobite cause, unlike the Geordies farther south at Newcastle.

A rich countryside

Despite and indeed perhaps even because of such unrest, this corner is one of the most rewarding in Britain, a landscape infused with echoes of the past. Unrest, uncertainty and remoteness have it devoid of sprawling development and instead, small towns, quiet villages and scattered farming settlements are the norm. Within its bounds lie the Northumberland Coast and part of the North Pennines AONBs, two National Scenic Areas: Upper Tweedale and Eildon and Leaderfoot, as well as the whole of the Northumberland National Park. In addition there are countless other areas of natural, geological and historic interest including the extensive Kielder Forest Park and of course Hadrian's Wall. Nowhere is the scenery less than stunning and the loveliness of nature is to be found all around.

Exploring the landscape

There is no shortage of superb walking within the borders as evidenced by the web of long-distance routes that criss-cross the countryside. Britain's first National Trail, the Pennine Way culminates in a traverse of the Cheviot Hills to end at Kirk Yetholm, while the most recent, Hadrian's Wall Path opened in 2003 and has become immediately popular. The Scottish equivalent is the Long Distance Route and over the border lies the Southern Upland Way. All of these are touched by the walks included here, and may inspire you to take up the challenge of completing one or all of them in their entirety. In addition there are more than 40 long-distance paths on both sides of the border, which are promoted by the county and local councils. These range from 14 to 200 miles and include the Alternative Coast to Coast, the Reivers Way, the John Buchan Way, St Cuthbert's Way, St Oswald's Way and the Borders Abbeys Way. Indeed a couple of real leg stretchers pass through too, the Great English Walk at 623 miles and the 1,243-mile North Sea Trail. But for most people a less demanding half or full day's walk is sufficient and the routes gathered here explore some of the area's most impressive landscapes.

The diversity of the coast is revealed in walks contrasting the soaring, sheer cliffs and stacks of St Abb's Head with the low sea-washed shelves and rocks around Craster. Castles and monastic houses studded the length of the coast, but nowhere are they more dramatically brought together than the tranquil Holy Island of Lindisfarne, cut off from the mainland twice a day by the tide.

Hills range throughout the region and, although they are not high compared with many others across the British Isles, they are among the loneliest. Their untamed beauty is enhanced by their solitude, very often there is hardly a sign of human habitation and you might not see another person all day. Several walks explore the rolling uplands and long, winding valleys of the Cheviot Hills, including the most challenging route within the book, a roundabout circuit to the top of The Cheviot itself.

Scattered throughout the region are relics of man's presence since the Stone Age. A stone circle and enigmatic rock carvings are to be found on the moor above Doddington, while hillforts are passed on several walks. One of the most visually impressive sites stands in the Whiteadder Valley where a broch and hut circles overlie an earlier fortification.

One of the most visited parts of the border region is Hadrian's Wall, built in the first century to define and protect the northern limit of the Roman Empire. The central section crosses the watershed of England, where it passes through the wildest and most rugged terrain of its course. But this stretch also contains the best-preserved portions of wall and a number of impressive forts and other structures. Four walks string together the finest segments, providing a vivid image of the scale of the undertaking and the way in which it must have dominated the landscape and peoples of its day.

The 19th century saw a massive expansion of railways across the kingdom, and many of the villages and small towns of the Scottish borders were connected with the outside world for the first time. Snaking along the valleys of the Tweed, Teviot and others, they were among the most picturesque routes in the country. Although closed during the 1950s and 60s, many continue as footpaths and cycle routes, some of which are encountered along the walks here.

The area's small towns scattered along the valleys each display an individuality of character, a lively heart and are steeped in history. Melrose has its abbey, one of the foremost religious foundations in Scotland as does Kelso, while all are founded on an attractively practical architecture that developed after the Union and shows similarities on both sides of the border.

A number of routes have been included simply for the stunning beauty of the countryside through which they pass; the Victorian woodland garden of Allen Banks, the superb viewpoint of Peniel Heugh and the grand hill walk of Arnton Fell. Other walks hark back to something of the area's heritage; the lead mining that took place around one of England's prettiest villages, Blanchland or St Cuthbert's Cave, a stop along the wandering journey taken by the monks of Lindisfarne. However, the collection, while illustrating the tremendous diversity that the region has to offer can only scratch the surface and leaves plenty of scope for further exploration.

The walks

The walks are grouped into three categories, beginning with the shorter circuits and progressing to those which present more of a challenge. The ranking considers overall distance, but also takes into account the height gain, terrain and degree of isolation. Some of the rambles venture into areas that are less frequented and thus made more challenging simply because, in the event of an accident, it is unlikely that there will be anyone nearby to give assistance.

The guide time is an indication of how long a reasonably fit person might take to complete the walk under fair weather conditions, but makes no allowance for stops or the extra effort needed in bad weather. Snow and ice will obviously slow the pace, but rain and boggy ground also make the going much harder. A brief description of the terrain adds to the information you can derive from the map in assessing the nature of the ground and you should also take account of the fitness and experience of your party in planning your day.

By and large, the routes are directed along discernible paths and tracks that are generally waymarked. However, on the open hill, waymarks and cairns are often infrequent and paths can be vague or occasionally non-existent. Navigation in these areas, particularly in poor weather can be difficult *and walkers who are competent and confident in the use of both map and compass should only undertake such walks*. Ordnance Survey maps complement the sections of mapping provided within this guide and while the Landranger series is useful in determining your position in relation to more distant landmarks, Explorer maps contain significantly more detail for plotting your route. GPS provides an added dimension to finding your way about the countryside and co-ordinates are provided for the waypoints. These can be invaluable in helping determine a position under adverse conditions, but GPS should be regarded as an addition to conventional navigation techniques and not a substitute.

This book covers a vast area of countryside where change is inevitable. The lines of paths occasionally alter, while some are lost and new ones created. As forest plantations mature, they become ready for harvesting, an operation that can result in temporary closure or re-routing of paths. Notices warn of ongoing work and, for your own safety, you should follow posted instructions. This of course leads to a transformation of the landscape and opens new views. Sometimes the land is left to regenerate naturally or planted as woodland to regain native tree cover. Elsewhere commercial timber crops are replanted, but now often include a diversity of species rather than the monoculture often practised in the past.

This book includes a list of waypoints alongside the description of the walk, so that you can enjoy the full benefits of gps should you wish to. For more information on using your gps, read the *Pathfinder® Guide GPS for Walkers*, by gps teacher and navigation trainer, Clive Thomas (ISBN 978-0-7117-4445-5). For essential information on map reading and basic navigation, read the *Pathfinder® Guide Map Reading Skills* by outdoor writer, Terry Marsh (ISBN 978-0-7117-4978-8). Both titles are available in bookshops or can be ordered online at www.totalwalking.co.uk

Kielder Water – the Bull Crag Peninsula

		GPS waypoints
Start	Bull Crag Peninsula, signed from road along forest track	✐ NY 677 870
Distance	3 miles (4.8km)	Ⓐ NY 675 872
Height gain	280 feet (85m)	Ⓑ NY 688 869
Approximate time	1½ hours	Ⓒ NY 676 865
Parking	Otterstone Viewpoint car park	
Route terrain	Clear tracks and paths	
Ordnance Survey maps	Landranger 80 (Cheviot Hills & Kielder Water), Explorer OL42 (Kielder Water & Forest – Bellingham & Simonside Hills)	

This is an excellent, undemanding lakeside walk, particularly suitable for families with younger children, who can look for small brass panels set along the way. The plaques are ideal for making brass rubbings, so remember to include crayons and squares of paper within the picnic pack. The route follows good forest tracks and clear paths around this picturesquely set tongue of land protruding into the lake.

The last century saw two great changes in what had predominantly been the bare upper reaches of the River North Tyne; the planting of a huge state forest, the most extensive in England and, more recently, the construction of a massive dam to create the largest reservoir in Britain. Kielder has become

Kielder Water from the Otterstone Viewpoint

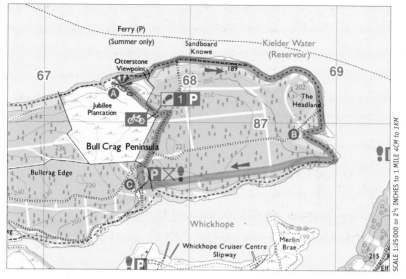

SCALE 1:25000 or 2½ INCHES to 1 MILE 4CM to 1KM

| 0 | 200 | 400 | 600 | 800 METRES | 1 |
| 0 | 200 | 400 | 600 YARDS | ½ | KILOMETRES MILES |

one of the most popular outdoor activity areas in the country offering countless opportunities for walking, cycling and boating. The forest habitat supports a huge variety of wildlife, including one of England's largest red squirrel populations and lately, breeding ospreys, an event not seen in Northumberland for over 200 years. Among other animals you might spot are roe deer and bats, and keep an eye open for birds such as hen harriers, goshawk and barn owls.

One of the brass panels lies at the start of the walk as the path leaves the far side of the car park. It leads to a kissing-gate from which there is the first of many superb views across Kielder Water. The path continues across open grassland before dropping through a second kissing-gate onto a broad path above the shore **A**.

Follow the Lakeside Way to the right, which soon winds into the forest cloaking the snout of the Bull Crag Peninsula. It meanders through the fringe of the trees before emerging, quite surprisingly, upon a stretch of tarmac road complete with line markings. It is a remnant of the valley road before it was flooded beneath the reservoir in 1982. A railway ran along the other side of the valley and that too has disappeared. The dam that wrought the change upon the landscape can be seen straight ahead, a massive embankment more than ¾ mile long and 170 feet high, blocking off the valley.

Where the road dips into the water, bear right to pick up the resumption of the track. It describes a serpentine course above the shore, eventually rounding a point to sweep back into the head of a small inlet **B**. Carry on around a second promontory before turning in above the broad estuary of Cranecleugh Burn, which is used as moorings for boats below a marina on the opposite shore. Undulating at a high level above the lake, the track reveals some lovely views through the trees.

The trail eventually ends at a junction of broad tracks **C**. There turn right, climbing to a second junction and go right again, now on the main forest road. Keep ahead and then left at subsequent junctions to return to the car park. ●

Blanchland

Start	Blanchland
Distance	3½ miles (5.6km)
Height gain	525 feet (160m)
Approximate time	2 hours
Parking	Car park in village
Route terrain	Clear tracks, woodland paths
Ordnance Survey maps	Landranger 87 (Hexham & Haltwhistle), Explorers OL43 (Hadrian's Wall – Haltwhistle & Hexham) and 307 (Consett & Derwent Reservoir)

GPS waypoints

✎ NY 964 504
Ⓐ NY 963 509
Ⓑ NY 949 517
Ⓒ NY 958 499

Despite many preconceptions, the north of England has its fair share of unspoiled towns and villages, and few would disagree with Blanchland's claim to being one of the most picturesque. It nestles in a lovely wooded fold amid the bleak moors of the North Pennines AONB, a superb beginning for this fine walk connecting the sheltered valleys of Shildon Burn and the upper River Derwent.

Blanchland was founded in 1165 for the Premonstratensian order, originally as a priory, but later elevated under the rule of an abbot. It was from the White Canons that the place derived its name. Ever only a small community set amid wild surroundings, life in the abbey appears to have been fairly austere and disrupted from time to time by border raiders. Local tales tell of one marauding band that became disoriented by the moorland mist and bypassed the abbey. But, the monks, in an over-eager celebration of their deliverance rang the bells, bringing back the raiders who were, unfortunately, still wandering about within earshot. Despite a short reprieve because of its usefulness as a hostel for travellers in this remote corner, the abbey was dissolved in 1539. The church was adapted for parish services and the guests' lodgings taken as a manor house. After he bought the estate in 1704, Lord Crewe, Bishop of Durham, built the village we see today to house his lead miners. On his death, he included the estate within a charitable trust and is remembered in the name of the village pub, fittingly set within what remains of the old abbey guest house.

✎ Out of the car park, turn right but then almost at once go left and left again onto a rising track that is signed as a footpath. After climbing at the backs of cottages it swings into the woods behind the village. Ignore a path shortly branching off right and keep ahead up a sunken track to join a broader, green trail.

Descending gently to the left, watch for a path soon leaving discretely on the right Ⓐ. Where it immediately splits at a waypost, take the left branch, passing out of the trees through a small gate. Walk away above the wood at the edge of rough grazing, dropping at the far end into a leafy corner, where humps and hollows remain from old lead mines. Leaving at a gate, continue along a green track. Keep right through a gate in front of a cottage and follow a track out to the end of a lane.

Lead has been mined in the area since at least medieval times, evidenced by the numerous hollows of collapsed bell pits in the area. During the 19th century, the improved techniques of the Industrial Age allowed deeper mining. The ruins beside the burn opposite the settlement centre on an engine house from this period, which was used for pumping water from the lower levels. The farm at the top of the hill apparently got its name from selling penny pies to miners walking to their work.

The route lies to the right, passing several of the old mine shafts fenced off in the trees on its way to Pennypie House, ¾ mile up the hill. As the track swings up to the farm, keep ahead through a gate **B** onto the open moor,

but then immediately turn left across a bridge spanning the burn, the way signed to Baybridge.

A sandy track hugs the wall at the edge of the heather moor and gives good views across the head of the Derwent Valley for the next ¾ mile. Eventually joining a track from a screened gas pumping station, leave the moor and follow a lane downhill beside a wood.

At the bottom, go right on the main lane past the Baybridge picnic area. Just before reaching a bridge across the River Derwent, abandon the lane for a footpath on the left signed to Blanchland and Carrick **C**. A short length of duckboarding conducts you to the riverbank, where a very pretty path follows the crystal water as it babbles over a bouldery bed, overhung with trees. All too soon the path reaches Blanchland Bridge. Walk out to the lane and turn left back into the village. ●

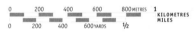

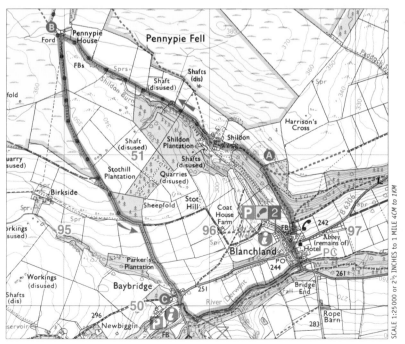

Doddington Moor

Start	Doddington
Distance	4 miles (6.4km)
Height gain	540 feet (165m)
Approximate time	2 hours
Parking	Lay-by south of Doddington village cross or off main road in one of the side lanes
Route terrain	Heathland paths and lane
Ordnance Survey maps	Landranger 75 (Berwick-upon-Tweed), Explorer 340 (Holy Island & Bamburgh)

GPS waypoints

🖉 NT 999 323
Ⓐ NU 016 333
Ⓑ NU 013 323
Ⓒ NU 013 317
Ⓓ NU 012 313
Ⓔ NU 004 316

The route begins from Doddington Cross along a country lane, which gives a fine prospect to the far off hills, before climbing onto the moor in search of its prehistoric relics. The final stretch looks out to the Cheviot Hills and peers down upon the hamlet, where its ruined 16th-century bastle remains a prominent feature.

When Britain basked in a warmer climate than today, Doddington Moor was well populated with Bronze Age peoples who farmed the hillsides. They left their marks across what has now become heath in countless carvings upon the rocks, strange shapes known as 'cup and ring' marks. Relatively recent is the imposing cross set back from the road in the centre of the village. It stands above a natural spring, Dod Well and was designed by the local vicar in 1846.

🖉 Leave the main road beside the cross along a narrow lane signed to the Wooler Golf Club. Climbing gently away, it gives a view to the distant Lammermuir Hills of Scotland. Where the lane eventually swings towards the golf club, keep ahead on an undulating sandy track.

Pass a large cattle shed and later go through a gate to dip beside a small plantation. Some 150 yds beyond the wood leave through a gate on the right Ⓐ. Strike sharp right across the cultivation in the direction indicated by the fingerpost to Weetwood Hill, on a bearing just west of south. Maintain the direction across the next rising pasture to a gate in the far corner.

Through that, follow the wall towards a clump of pine. As you approach the trees, look back right to a low bracken-covered hill. Ramparts and ditches surround the top, an Iron Age fort that continued as a settlement site into the Roman period. Ignoring the clearer path that then bears off to the right Ⓑ, remain beside the wall. Over a stile pass onto bracken moor, accompanying the wall to a single standing stone Ⓒ. It is the sole survivor of a stone circle – the others lie fallen in the undergrowth.

Keep going over the crest, eventually reaching a corner with a fence Ⓓ. Turn

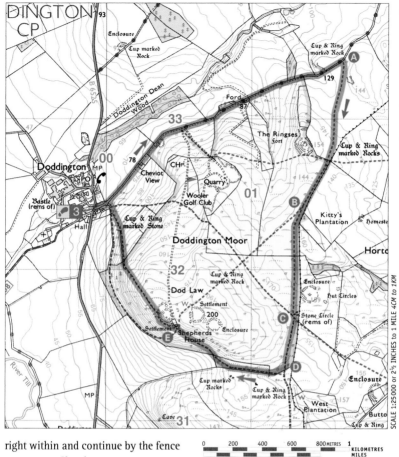

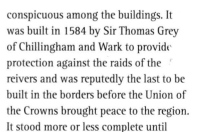

right within and continue by the fence past a gate. Shortly, a cottage comes into view on the hillside in the middle distance. A waymark indicates a path leaving the fence, which rises across the slope of the hill. Mount a stile in an intervening boundary and continue below a low scar to the cottage, Shepherds House **E**.

Some of the most intriguing stone carvings on the moor are to be found around the summit of the hill behind Shepherds House. Follow the track up beside its boundary wall and then explore the ground beyond over to the right.

Return to the cottage and now go right on a bracken trod to resume your line along the flank of the hill. Before long, the path begins to fall towards the village, the tall ruin of the bastle

conspicuous among the buildings. It was built in 1584 by Sir Thomas Grey of Chillingham and Wark to provide protection against the raids of the reivers and was reputedly the last to be built in the borders before the Union of the Crowns brought peace to the region. It stood more or less complete until 1896, when a severe gale brought down the eastern end. Over a fence, follow a sparse line of hawthorn trees, holding your direction beyond its end. Breaking from the bracken, drop across pasture and then between clumps of gorse to find a stile at the bottom. Regaining the golf club lane, follow it left back to the village.

●

Peniel Heugh

		GPS waypoints
Start	Harestanes Visitor Centre, 1 mile east of Ancrum	📍 NT 641 244
Distance	4½ miles (7.2km)	Ⓐ NT 644 246
Height gain	625 feet (190m)	Ⓑ NT 647 254
Approximate time	2 hours	Ⓒ NT 653 263
Parking	Car park Harestanes Visitor Centre	Ⓓ NT 645 265
Route terrain	Lanes, tracks and woodland paths	Ⓔ NT 638 258
Ordnance Survey maps	Landranger 74 (Kelso & Coldstream), Explorer OL16 (The Cheviot Hills)	Ⓕ NT 644 248

The circuit climbs to the stunning viewpoint of Peniel Heugh, where a striking monument remembers the Battle of Waterloo. A roundabout return through woodland and along quiet lanes eventually joins St Cuthbert's Way, passing a delightful walled garden before returning to Harestanes.

📍 Walk out to the lane, going left and left again. Just past the high wall of Harestanes, pick up a parallel footpath on the left. Curve with it around the field corner to cross a plank bridge, briefly accompanying the stream before swinging up steps onto a wider path Ⓐ.

Follow it left into woodland, shortly passing a small wildlife pond. Keep ahead past a junction, shortly meeting a tarmac drive. To the right is Monteviot House, seat of the marquesses of Lothian, whose gardens are open to the public. The route, however, rises left to a road, continuing along the drive opposite. Approaching the gamekeeper's house, fork right onto a grass track, going right again after 50 yds onto a narrower path climbing at the edge of trees to a lane Ⓑ.

Go right and almost immediately left onto a rising woodland trail. Keep left at successive forks, higher up being rewarded with a sudden glimpse of the summit tower. As the gradient eases, bear right at a fork to leave the wood through a kissing-gate. Beyond a second kissing-gate, strike a beeline across open ground for the hilltop Ⓒ.

Rising 150 feet, the monument was erected by the sixth Marquess of Lothian to commemorate the Duke of Wellington's victory at Waterloo.

The Waterloo Monument on Peniel Heugh

Drop north onto a grass track that leads away to the right, almost immediately passing through a broken wall. Leave left on a trod, falling steeply below the wall towards the forest. Over a stile, a path descends steadily through the trees. Eventually meeting a track, go left out to a lane **D**.

Turn right to a junction and go left onto a long, straight lane. Crossing a bridge a few yards along, there is a fine view back to the hill, while farther on, a small loch to the right attracts geese, swans and other waterbirds. Follow the lane for ¾ mile then, shortly beyond a bend, look for a gap in the left wall **E**.

Marked St Cuthbert's Way, a path heads into the thick of the trees, its almost dead-straight course betraying Roman origins. It is in fact Dere Street, which ran for almost 200 miles between York and the Firth of Forth. In time, the way swings over a bridge spanning a stream. Ignore the crossing path and keep going above the burn, eventually crossing it again at a second bridge. A signpost just beyond invites a detour to **Woodside Walled Garden**, where the **tearoom** uses local produce for its appetising range of snacks and light meals.

Return to follow St Cuthbert's Way down to the road, crossing to the continuing path opposite. Approaching a bridge **F**, turn right to remain on this bank. A pleasant path winds through old woodland dominated by ancient beech, and finally swings left to the Harestanes Visitor Centre. ●

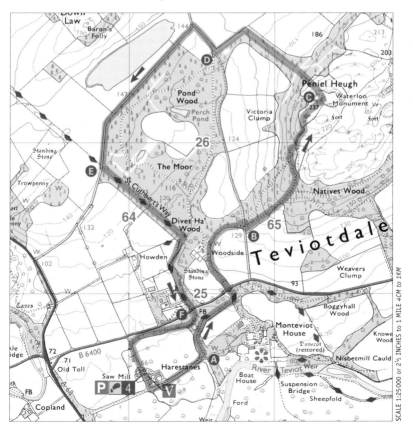

Allen Banks

		GPS waypoints
Start	Allen Banks, near Bardon Mill	
Distance	3½ miles (5.6km)	NY 798 639
Height gain	770 feet (235m)	Ⓐ NY 798 632
Approximate time	2 hours	Ⓑ NY 794 625
Parking	National Trust car park	Ⓒ NY 794 622
Route terrain	Some rough woodland paths and steep ground	Ⓓ NY 798 632
Ordnance Survey maps	Landrangers 86 (Haltwhistle & Brampton) or 87 (Hexham & Haltwhistle), Explorer OL43 (Hadrian's Wall – Haltwhistle & Hexham)	

The Honourable Francis Bowes Lyon gave the Victorian woodland garden of Allen Banks to the National Trust in 1942. It lies in a beautiful, richly arboreal valley enclosing one of the main tributaries of the River South Tyne, and is particularly attractive in early summer when carpeted with bluebells and ransoms.

Follow a path through the picnic area, beside the river into the wood. Go quietly and you might spot an otter in the water. Beyond a suspension bridge, climb to meet a higher path Ⓐ. Cross and continue the upward trend, slanting more steeply across the wooded bank and eventually zigzagging up the final stretch. Broaching the top, walk on to a

Looking from the summerhouse into the gorge

summerhouse. Several such bowers were scattered around the valley, where the family could relax and appreciate spectacular views along the river. The one here contains a 'book' portraying the history of the estate.

Bear right on a level and easy path along the rim of the valley. Splendid beech trees that are at their best when the leaves turn in autumn border the ride here. After a while, the path leads to the site of another summerhouse, perched above the deep ravine of Hoods Burn, which falls into the main valley. Although the structure is long gone, the mosaic floor remains, apparently fashioned from the knucklebones of sheep.

An orange waymark indicates the way dropping left. *Partly stepped, it is steep and demands care during wet weather.* Rejoining the main riverside trail Ⓑ, follow it over a plank bridge spanning Hoods Burn. After a small meadow, the path delves into the Briarwood Banks Nature Reserve, an ancient woodland of oak, ash and hazel coppice. Keep left at a fork crossing a side stream to a robust bridge spanning the River Allen ⓒ. It replaces a suspension bridge that was washed away during a flood in 2005.

Beyond the bridge, bear right to a field gate at Plankey Mill. Swing left in front of a barn to climb away on a narrow lane. As it then bends, abandon it for a descending track, keeping left again when it splits to pass a ruined building. Just before it finishes, slip through a kissing-gate on the left from which a contained path runs beside a meadow. At the end, drop to continue along the riverbank.

Over a stile and footbridge, the path follows the river into a gorge, picking a rising course among a litter of boulders. Ignore an unsigned path off right but as the way then levels, watch for a fork. A black waymark guides you right, climbing above the river. When you later reach another junction, keep ahead to find a purple waymarked path branching up steps, a few yards farther along on the right ⓓ.

Cresting a rise, it falls to a crossing path where The Tarn is signed to the right. Resume the climb to another crossing and this time go left up steps. There is a view across the River South Tyne Valley before, a little lower down, The Tarn suddenly appears in front of you. Surrounded by trees, it occupies an idyllically picturesque spot.

Joining a broader path, pass left of

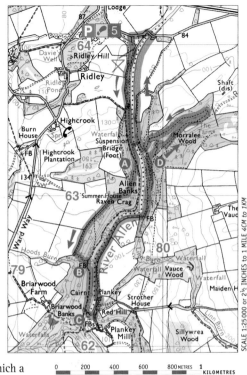

SCALE 1:25000 or 2½ INCHES to 1 MILE 4CM to 1KM

the pool. At the far end, look out for another purple waypost from which a narrow path bears left. Over a low rise, it doubles back in easy descent across the wooded slope of the hill, eventually returning you to the crossing passed on the way up.

Still following purple waymarks, turn right. At the next junction go left and then left again to come upon the steps by which you began the ascent to The Tarn. Now swing sharp right, losing height steeply to meet the River Allen at a suspension bridge. You can either cross and retrace your outward route or alternatively, continue downstream on this bank. Leaving the wood carry on at the edge of a couple of meadows, ultimately approaching a bridge. Walk beneath it and then turn up to the lane, which leads across the river back to the car park. ●

Craster and Dunstanburgh Castle

		GPS waypoints
Start	Craster	✏ NU 256 198
Distance	4¾ miles (7.6km)	Ⓐ NU 257 213
Height gain	380 feet (115m)	Ⓑ NU 245 224
Approximate time	2 hours	Ⓒ NU 250 207
Parking	Car park at edge of village (Pay and Display)	
Route terrain	Well-used paths	
Ordnance Survey maps	Landrangers 75 (Berwick-upon-Tweed) and 81 (Alnwick & Morpeth), Explorer 332 (Alnwick & Amble)	

The only downside to this walk is the justifiable popularity of the coastal path, which leads to one of Northumberland's most evocative castles. Early mornings or late evenings are quiet, when misty light and long shadows add their own special quality, but unfortunately the castle is then closed. The route cuts back across country over the fine vantage of The Heughs.

The aroma from Robson's smokehouse pervades the tiny fishing village, famous for its oak-smoked kippers and salmon. The Crasters have held the manor since 1272 and built the harbour in 1906, where herring were once landed. It is a memorial to Captain John Craster, killed on active service in Tibet.

✏ Follow the road from the car park to the harbour, there turning left past cottages. Through a gate at the end, a path continues above the sloping rocky shore towards the distant castle. The rocks trap countless pools from the receding tide, home to small crabs, shrimps and sea anemones. After two more gates Ⓐ, *the path splits, that ahead leading to the castle entrance.*

Begun around 1313 by Thomas, Earl of Lancaster, Dunstanburgh sits imposingly upon an outcrop of whinstone, part of the Great Whin Sill

volcanic intrusion. The formation curves through the north Pennines, underlies part of Hadrian's Wall and makes a final appearance off the coast as the Farne Islands. The castle's curtain walls enclose some nine acres, heightening the natural defences of the sea cliffs and steep inland bank that protect it on three sides. The entrance lies through an impressive gatehouse flanked by twin towers. The fortification remained impregnable until the Wars of the Roses, when it succumbed to the Earl of Warwick's pounding canon. Abandoned, it crumbled into the romantic ruin we see today.

Unless visiting the castle, bear left at the fork, passing through a marshy depression that sidesteps the castle hill. Once flooded, it provided a harbour for Henry VIII's fleet in 1514. The path winds beneath the western defences and

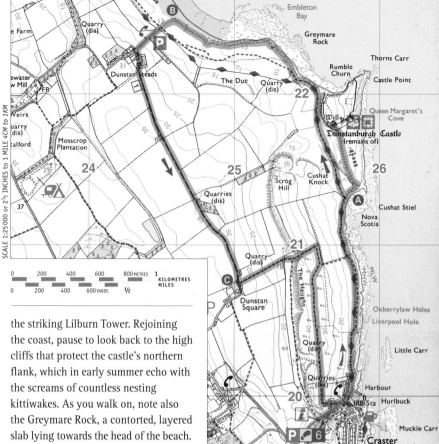

the striking Lilburn Tower. Rejoining the coast, pause to look back to the high cliffs that protect the castle's northern flank, which in early summer echo with the screams of countless nesting kittiwakes. As you walk on, note also the Greymare Rock, a contorted, layered slab lying towards the head of the beach.

Keep above the shore past the golf course, the sand hills hiding a couple of pill boxes, part of the coastal defences during the last war. Eventually, the dunes are broken by a gap **B**, through which a path runs from the beach across the golf course to the end of a lane.

Amble up to holiday cottages at Dunstan Steads, immediately before which, turn left through a gate. A drive winds around the buildings and past a barn, leaving through a gate at the far corner. Take the concrete track ahead across open fields, which gives a fine view to the castle before passing a copse of pine sheltering a large limekiln.

Reaching the farm at Dunstan Square, turn off opposite barns through a signposted gate on the left **C**. Walk away at the edge of a field ridged with

medieval ox ploughing, passing through another gate at the bottom to climb to a nick in The Heughs, the line of cliffs ahead. At the top, keep the same line beside a fence to the corner. Go through the gate on the right and walk away with the fence. Passing a second gate, bear off to take a parallel course some 50 yds to the right. Carry on as you later join another fence, Craster's cottages now appearing ahead. Over a stile, the ongoing path is contained by clumps of gorse behind the long gardens of the fishermen's cottages. At the end, swing left to meet a street, which falls into the village. The car park is then just a short distance away to the right. ●

Simonside

		GPS waypoints
Start	Simonside Forest Park, ¾ mile south east of Great Tosson	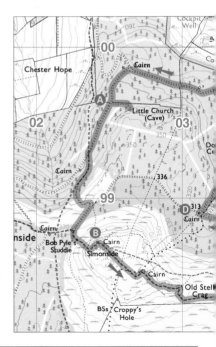 NZ 036 996
Distance	4½ miles (7.2km). Extension 2¾ miles (4.6km)	**A** NZ 025 996
Height gain	920 feet (280m). Extension 200 feet (60m)	**B** NZ 024 987
Approximate time	2½ hours. Extension 1½ hours	**C** NZ 038 985
Parking	Forest car park	**D** NZ 031 989
Route terrain	Woodland and heath paths, occasionally rugged	
Ordnance Survey maps	Landranger 81 (Alnwick & Morpeth), Explorer OL42 (Kielder Water & Forest – Bellingham & Simonside Hills)	

Although only 10 miles from the Cheviots, the Simonside Hills have a completely different character, rugged sandstone outcrops defining their summits. The walk climbs through the delightful forest of the lower slopes onto the most spectacular, although not quite the highest of the tops. This short ramble can be enjoyably extended along the ridge to an Iron Age fort upon a neighbouring hill.

Facing the information board at the car park entrance, take the track on the right. Walk past a barrier into the forest, picking up red waymarks that will act as a guide throughout the walk. Bear right at a fork and carry on to another split, there going right again past a TV booster transmitter. The track undulates through the trees, before long reaching another junction in a small clearing. Now go left, the way climbing once more. Through a barrier, look for a narrow path off left **A** which leads to Little Church Rock – a monolithic outcrop of the sandstone that underlies the hills. Its name harks back to the Reformation, when clandestine religious meetings were held in defiance of the established Church.

Return to the main trail and continue

for another ¼ mile to intercept a diagonal path. Follow it left into the trees shortly passing beneath another impressive outcrop. Nearby, the rock underfoot is inscribed with criss-cross grooves, possibly done by drovers to help prevent cattle from slipping as they were herded along the track.

Breaking from the trees, fork left and gain height across open heather moor towards the impressive rocky face of Simonside. Meeting another track, go right for some 200 yds to a waymark. There, branch left up a steep, scrambling path onto the upper hill, which although improved to combat erosion, remains a rugged climb.

The top is soon attained and your effort is rewarded with a spectacular view that remains throughout the next leg of the walk. From a large cairn marking a prehistoric burial **B**, a flagged path leads towards a second outcrop, winding right to gain its summit from the back. The path continues across the airy moor later descending from Old Stell Crag to Dove Crag, the site of another ancient burial. A stepped path leaves the top, reaching a waypost 150 yds below, **C**.

The extension continues along the path ahead, over the ladder-stile in the lower fence and on across The Beacon before descending to the lane opposite a small car park. The Iron Age fort extends over the rising ground beyond and several rocks bear intriguing cup and ring markings. You can then return to the forest car park, which lies to the north west, about a mile along the quiet lane.

Otherwise, go left, abandoning the stepped path at **C** and curving back below Dove Crag to drop from the heather through an area of felled forest. Reaching a T-junction, turn left and then at the next junction **D**, right to follow a descending forest track above Coe Burn. After ¼ mile, watch for a path forking off on the right that continues down through the trees. Carry on to the bottom and then swing left back to the car park. ●

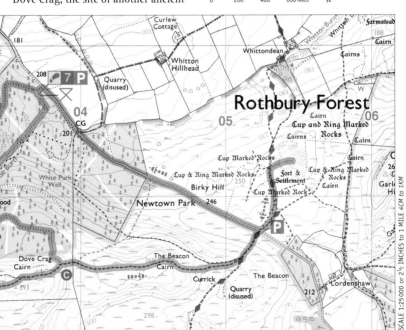

Hadrian's Wall from Steel Rigg

		GPS waypoints
Start	Steel Rigg, ¾ mile north of Once Brewed National Park Information Centre	🥾 NY 751 676 Ⓐ NY 780 686 Ⓑ NY 778 690 Ⓒ NY 771 684
Distance	4¾ miles (7.6km)	
Height gain	770 feet (235m)	
Approximate time	2½ hours	
Parking	Car park at start (Pay and Display)	
Route terrain	Rugged path along wall, short stretch across moor	
Ordnance Survey maps	Landrangers 86 (Haltwhistle & Brampton) or 87 (Hexham & Haltwhistle), Explorer OL43 (Hadrian's Wall – Haltwhistle & Hexham)	

This is, without doubt, one of the most dramatic sections of Hadrian's Wall and is justifiably popular with visitors. However relatively few venture far from the car park and are content merely to gaze along the line of cliffs that rear above Crag Lough. The walk continues over Hotbank Crags before dropping off to return across the rough northern pastures that foot the rearing sill.

The wall was the brainchild of Emperor Hadrian, who visited Britannia in 122 to inspect the northernmost province of his empire following a revolt among the Brigantes. His aim was to secure rather than expand the territory and he ordered the construction of a defence right across the country between the Tyne and Solway. Work began that same year and was largely complete by 128. When finished, it was 80 Roman miles long (73½ statute miles) with a gateway guarded by a fortlet or milecastle every mile.

Under Hadrian's successor, Antoninus Pius, the frontier was pushed farther north between the Forth and the Clyde, and in 142 a second wall was begun, now known as the Antonine Wall.

Although only half the length of Hadrian's Wall, it took twice as long to build. It was abandoned within 20 years and the frontier was once again fixed on Hadrian's line.

As well as being a strategic line of defence and awesome symbol of the might of the Roman Empire, the wall also served to regulate trade and the comings and goings of people across the frontier. The milecastles and forts served as customs posts where goods could be taxed, and civilian settlements grew up around the forts to take advantage of passing trade.

🖊 From a gate at the rear of the car park, a path leads to the line of the Roman wall. Go left into Peel Gap before climbing steeply to a ladder-stile at the

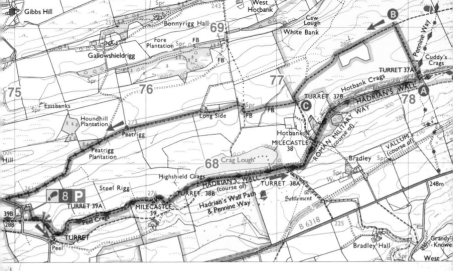

SCALE 1:27777 or 2½ INCHES to 1 MILE 3.6CM to 1KM

top of the crag. The strategic value of the setting is vividly demonstrated here in the lofty whinstone cliffs overlooking Crag Lough. The defence was virtually unassailable and provided a superb vantage commanding the rolling countryside to the north, which, despite their best efforts, the Romans had never fully been able to wrest from the control of the Caledonians.

Carry on beside the wall, which has been restored to an impressive shoulder height. In the next gap, known as Cat Stairs, wild flowers flourish in the poor soil, improved by lime that has leached from the crumbling mortar and infill. After another sharp climb, the way drops to Castle Nick, which is protected by one of the 80 milecastles that were originally planned along the length of the wall.

In the next dip, the path cuts through to the outer flank of the wall. Clamber up to continue high above Crag Lough before descending gently through pine woodland towards the far end of the lough. Leaving the trees, walk on to intersect a track leading to Hotbank Farm. Cross the wall and skirt the farm, climbing over Hotbank Crags to

Ranishaw Gap Ⓐ. Leave it there, mounting a stile beside a gate. Ignoring the Pennine Way sign, head straight out from the wall, following the course of a dilapidated field boundary to reach a substantial limekiln, ¼ mile away Ⓑ.

At that point, turn left, following a vague track along the top of a low escarpment. Passing a plantation, bear slightly left, shortly picking up a more distinct track that curves left to a gate at the end of a wall behind Hotbank Farm Ⓒ.

Instead of passing through, cross a ladder-stile over to the right and strike out across a large pasture. Keep going to the far side of a second field, where a fingerpost directs you right to another stile. Resume your westerly heading past Crag Lough, side-stepping an enclosure and a couple of farm sheds. Carry on beside the ongoing wall, the way later materialising as a track that rises beside Peatrigg Plantation. It then winds down into the base of the valley, eventually meeting a lane. Climb left back to the car park at Steel Rigg. ●

Whiteadder Valley and Edin's Hall Broch

Start	Abbey St Bathans
Distance	5 miles (8km)
Height gain	870 feet (265m)
Approximate time	2½ hours
Parking	Car park by Riverside Restaurant
Route terrain	Heath and field paths, lane and track
Ordnance Survey maps	Landranger 67 (Duns, Dunbar & Eyemouth), Explorer 346 (Berwick-upon-Tweed)

GPS waypoints

- NT 762 618
- Ⓐ NT 767 611
- Ⓑ NT 772 603
- Ⓒ NT 786 604
- Ⓓ NT 789 609
- Ⓔ NT 780 621

Few brochs exist outside the far north of Scotland and its islands – consequently Edin's Hall is something of an oddity. It is explored on this enjoyable walk along the valley of Whiteadder Water from Abbey St Bathans, returning by a pleasant country route to the north.

Despite the settlement's name, there never was an abbey. Rather, it was a small priory for Cistercian nuns, founded at the beginning of the 13th century by Ada, Countess of Dunbar. The place took its name from a 6th-century Irish monk from Iona, St Bathan, who supposedly founded a chapel here. The priory was destroyed by English troops in 1543 and its site has now been lost, although the small church, just up the road from the start of the walk contains a funeral effigy of a prioress.

🖉 Follow the lane south past a wood yard, gradually gaining height above the valley for ½ mile. Where the lane bends sharply right, abandon it for a footpath signed to Edin's Hall Ⓐ. Steps lead down beside the edge of Ellerburn Wood to a bridge. Turn briefly downstream before climbing over a shoulder to emerge from the trees. An obvious trod strikes across the open lower flank of Cockburn Law, gently rising above the Whiteadder Valley. After ½ mile, approaching a gate, swing left down to a second smaller gate and stile, over which, climb to the broch Ⓑ.

Occupying a commanding platform above a steep slope, the broch's structure is immediately apparent. Within the thickness of a massive dry-stone annular wall are several rooms and the remains of a staircase to a higher level. Originally it would have been at least two storeys high, the central area roofed over with timber beams. Built during the 1st century, it stands within an earlier extensive hill fort, whose double ditch and earth rampart defences are readily discernible. Later occupation of the site is revealed in several hut circles, some of which overlie the earlier structures and probably date to the Roman period during the 2nd century.

Beyond the broch, the path falls across the hillside to a kissing-gate at the bottom end of a wall. Carry on at the edge of grazing above a steep wooded bank, crossing a couple of wall stiles before the path slants down to a lower pasture. Joining its left fence, continue above the river. In time, thorns squeeze the way to a gate, through which, the path drops to a track. Cross and continue behind a house to a bridge suspended above a rapid , which impressively churns the peaty flow of Whiteadder Water after heavy rain.

A track winds away between the trees, climbing beside Otter Burn. Reaching a lane at the top **D** go left. Follow it uphill for a mile, shortly leaving the woodland behind. Arriving at a junction **E**, go left to Blackerstone

The impressive remains of Edin's Hall Broch

and The Retreat, but after ¼ mile, where the lane then swings left, keep ahead on a broad track. It eventually meanders down to run at the edge of Butterwell Wood. Keep going for another ¼ mile before leaving over a stile on the right. Signed to Abbey St Bathans, a clear path rises through the bracken and gorse of the hillside, before dropping into trees to meet a track bringing the Southern Upland Way from Cockburnpath to the river. Cross a bridge beside the ford to go back to the car park.   ●

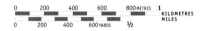

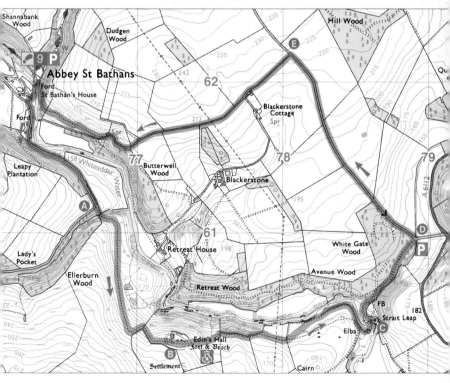

Arnton Fell

		GPS waypoints
Start	Second lay-by on right along unclassified lane, signed to Steele Road off B6399	📷 NY 514 932 🅐 NY 524 950 🅑 NY 529 965 🅒 NY 525 965 🅓 NY 516 951
Distance	5 miles (8km)	
Height gain	1,115 feet (340m)	
Approximate time	2½ hours	
Parking	Limited roadside parking, *do not obstruct passing place*	
Route terrain	Pathless moorland fell; *Note: hillside closed between April 10 – May 1 during lambing*	
Dog friendly	Dogs should be on leads at all times	
Ordnance Survey maps	Landranger 79 (Hawick & Eskdale), Explorer OL42 (Kielder Water & Forest – Bellingham & Simonside Hills)	

Arnton Fell is seemingly remote from anywhere, although until 40 years ago, the famous Waverley Line between Edinburgh and Carlisle ran below its eastern flank. The ascent of Arnton from the south and traverse of its broad, grassy ridge onto Blackwood Hill is rewarded by a superb view of Liddesdale and the hills that surround its head. Inexperienced walkers should choose a clear day.

📷 A stile beside a field gate opposite the lay-by gives access to the hillside. Ignore the gate ahead and instead bear left on a faint track paralleling a fence beginning on the right. Close with the fence farther up to pass a small plantation, going through a gate and steadily gaining height along the spur of the hill. Where the fence eventually swings right, break left, climbing more steeply to discover a triangulation pillar marking the end of the ridge. Isolated from the forest cloaking the eastern slope of the fell, it enjoys a magnificent panorama over the surrounding hills. To the west is Hermitage Castle, built in the 13th century to control one of the most fought-over valleys in the central borders. From here, it is much less forbidding than its reputation and perhaps suggests a visit later in the day.

With the strenuous part of the ascent now behind you, continue along the ridge towards a gateway and pile of stones, which marks the first high point 🅐. A rough path carries on for a generous mile beside the forest boundary, dipping gently before climbing to the somewhat higher summit of Blackwood Hill. Keep going beyond, descending to the corner of the fence 🅑.

Strike away, almost due west towards the distant castle. Descend steeply over rough ground to a grass track contouring the base of the hill 🅒.

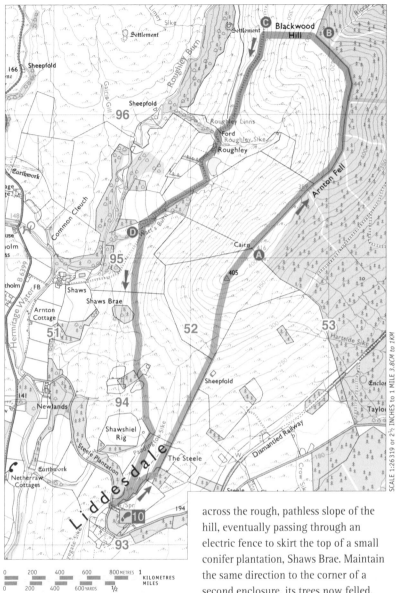

SCALE 1:26319 or 2½ INCHES to 1 MILE 3.8CM to 1KM

Follow it left for ½ mile, ultimately fording a stream by Roughley Farm. Now metalled, the track continues along the valley for another ½ mile before fording Watt's Burn.

As the track then curves away **D**, branch left at a shallow angle, rising across the grassy hillside above the hollow of a small shale quarry. Carry on across the rough, pathless slope of the hill, eventually passing through an electric fence to skirt the top of a small conifer plantation, Shaws Brae. Maintain the same direction to the corner of a second enclosure, its trees now felled.

Again cross an electric strand and briefly follow a fence on the right. When that turns down, keep ahead, later passing the tip of yet another plantation. Cross a gate there and bear right, now walking below the start of your outward route. Gradually close with the upper boundary of Steele Plantation over to the right and return to the lane. ●

Above Rothbury

		GPS waypoints
Start	Rothbury	🥾 NU 050 015
Distance	5¼ miles (8.5km)	Ⓐ NU 046 017
Height gain	820 feet (250m)	Ⓑ NU 046 020
Approximate time	2½ hours	Ⓒ NU 046 032
Parking	Beggars Rigg car park, ¼ mile west of Rothbury along B6341	Ⓓ NU 060 033
		Ⓔ NU 056 032
Route terrain	Heathland paths	Ⓕ NU 054 024
Ordnance Survey maps	Landranger 81 (Alnwick & Morpeth), Explorer 332 Alnwick & Amble)	

Rothbury clusters around a bridge over the River Coquet, its attractive setting belying a troubled past during the centuries of Border unrest. The walk begins from a riverside park and explores part of the open heath and forest of the Cragside estate before returning through the old heart of Rothbury and along the riverbank.

🥾 Leave the car park past a viewing platform to reach the road above. Follow it towards the town, but then turn back sharp left opposite Rothbury House, opened in 1789 as a private hotel. Follow the lane up the hill, continuing for another 400 yds after it levels to find steps set into the wall on the right beside the entrance drive of 'Midmar' Ⓐ. A path runs between the houses, curving left to tackle the steep wooded bank behind.

Reaching the top, mount a ladder-stile at the end of a wall. Keep ahead below an outcrop before passing into open pasture. Do not go through the gate behind a cottage, Gimmerknowe, instead turn right and follow a developing grass track beside the wall. Meeting a gravel track Ⓑ, turn left along it, later passing a house, Whinhams at Brae Head.

Rising beyond, the track curves to join a wall. After passing a gate through

which Physic Lane emerges from the left, track and wall diverge. Keep going past a clump of trees behind another short section of wall and, where the track then forks, take the left branch. Carry on across the heather moor over a shallow rise to intersect a more pronounced crossing track Ⓒ.

Go left, the way soon bending around to the northeast and drawing beside a stone wall. After briefly following its course, the track moves away into woodland. Shortly reaching a crossing track, go through the field gate opposite, the way signed to Primrose Cottage. The trail gently descends at the edge of the wood overlooking a picturesque valley.

At Primrose Cottage Ⓓ, turn right through a gate into Primrose Wood. Climb away for ¼ mile to a junction where a track is signed left to Rothbury. It undulates through the trees, the conifers relieved by birch and beech.

After another ¼ mile, just beyond a junction on the right, look out for a narrow path bearing off left  and dropping to a small gate. A clear path leads away over a footbridge across an expanse of sandy heath. After crossing a boggy stream, it rises towards the edge of Addyheugh Wood, there meeting a stony track emerging from the trees ➊.

Cross to the continuing path opposite, which follows the forest fence. After a few yards, you can deviate onto the hill for the fine panorama across the Coquet Valley to the Simonside Hills. Return to the path and wander downhill at the edge of the forest, eventually reaching a stile off the heath.

A contained path drops between house gardens to a street. Carry on downhill to a junction. Turn right and almost immediately left to pick up another path. At the bottom of that, go left and right along a final passageway that ends in the centre of Rothbury.

Cross to the street opposite and walk down past the church. Where it bends sharply left, keep ahead along a path beside the old Haa-Hill burial ground. It occupies the site of Rothbury Castle, which apparently remained occupied until the 1850s but then became ruinous and was pulled down to create extra burial space for the parish. The graveyard contains a number of noteworthy memorials, including the

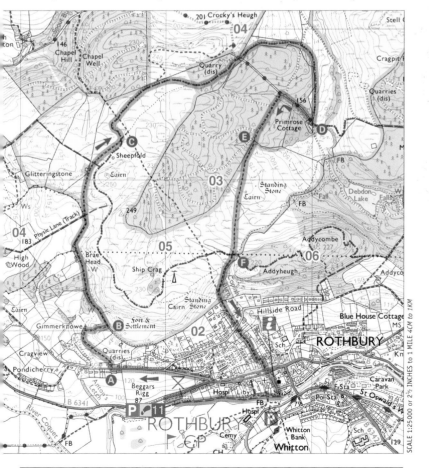

The track near Brae Head

Armstrong family tomb.

Born at Newcastle in 1810, William George Armstrong began his professional life as a solicitor. But his real interest lay in engineering, and his early work centred on hydraulics and electricity generation. After designing a crane for use in the shipyards he opened his own factory in 1847. The entrepreneur turned his attentions to bridge construction and armaments and was knighted for his design of an accurate breech-loading field gun. He subsequently turned to the manufacture of naval guns and then warships. In 1863, Armstrong began building Cragside above Rothbury, a place he had often visited as a child. He later restored the castle at Bamburgh and was a great benefactor to his own city, Newcastle, founding the origins of the university and supporting the building of the Hancock Museum.

Drop to a riverside path and follow it upstream. Reaching the picnic area, climb the bank to the car park above. ●

Lindisfarne

		GPS waypoints
Start	Holy Island	✐ NU 125 425
Distance	5½ miles (8.8km)	Ⓐ NU 119 435
Height gain	195 feet (60m)	Ⓑ NU 139 436
Approximate time	2½ hours	Ⓒ NU 129 419
Parking	Car park at edge of village (Pay and Display)	Ⓓ NU 125 419
Route terrain	Coastal paths, rocky beaches and sand dunes *Note: Consult tide-tables to check safe crossing times*	
Ordnance Survey maps	Landranger 75 (Berwick-upon-Tweed), Explorer 340 (Holy Island and Bamburgh)	

An Irish monk, Saint Aidan, brought Christianity to the kingdom of Northumbria in 635, founding a monastery on Lindisfarne under the patronage of King Oswald. Today, cut off twice a day by the tide, the tiny island remains a special place, rich in both wildlife and historical remains. There is much to see and it is worth spending a full day on the island.

Aidan's purpose was to take Christianity to Northumbria, and coming from Iona, chose the seclusion of this island upon which to establish his monastic retreat. After 17 years as Bishop, Aidan died at Bamburgh and was later succeeded by Cuthbert, a young shepherd boy who had been inspired by a vision of Aidan's soul rising to heaven. Cuthbert was renowned for his piety and generosity to the poor, but in later life sought the solitude of the Farne Islands. While there, he decreed protection for the nesting eider ducks, which today are known locally as *Cuddy Ducks*. After his death in 687 he was interred at Lindisfarne, but when his casket was opened 11 years later, his corpse was found to be preserved and miracles were attributed to him. When the community abandoned the island in the face of raiding Vikings, they took his body with them. After many long years of

wandering via Melrose, Chester-le-Street and Ripon, Cuthbert's body was finally laid to rest at Durham.

✐ From the northern end of the car park, walk back along the lane towards the shore, leaving before the bend through a signposted gate for a path at the edge of the dunes. Where it splits beyond the fields, keep ahead, passing the remains of a limekiln. Gaining height across the dunes, a view opens over the island. Maintain direction towards the northern coast, shortly encountering a ruin Ⓐ. Pass it on the right to find a gap in a cattle fence and walk out to the shore.

Turn right behind a sandy beach, which soon gives way to the low rocky slabs of Back Skerrs. In places smooth, elsewhere fractured, eroded and littered with boulders, the wave-washed rocks are of carboniferous sandstone, shale and limestone, the strata gently undulating as if emulating the swell of the sea. Hollows steal water from the receding tide wherein lurk tiny creatures, while barnacles and seaweeds coat the rocks.

Rounding the point brings you to the small, sandy bay of Coves Haven, sheltered by low cliffs at the far side. At low tide you can pick your way across the boulders, *but at high water you must resort to a path along the top*. Beyond Castlehead Rocks is a much larger bay, split by the reef of Keel Head extending into the sea.

Abandon the shore for the dunes as you approach a pyramidal navigation marker on Emmanuel Head **B**, exchanging views past Berwick to Scotland for a panorama to the south; a flashing lighthouse on Longstone marks the archipelago of the Farne Islands, while Bamburgh Castle and closer to, Lindisfarne Castle majestically perch on rocky outcrops.

Turning down the eastern coast, the going is easier on the grass above the bouldery apron of shore. Carry on over a stile and through a gate, the island's only lake lying over to the right. Known simply as The Lough, it attracts over-wintering waterfowl, particularly the pale-bellied brent goose. Eventually an elevated pathway curves toward the castle. It carried a tramway transporting limestone to a massive kiln on the left, well preserved and best seen from the bottom.

The impressive fort, built around 1540 to protect the harbour, was used

Unloading lobster pots in the harbour below Lindisfarne Castle

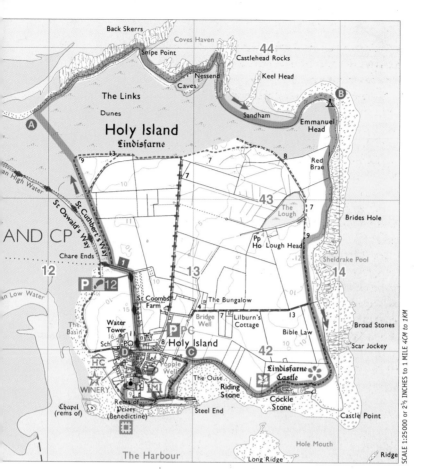

by troops sent to quell border uprisings. It was bought by the publisher Edward Hudson in 1901 who commissioned his friend, Edwin Lutyens to transform it into a comfortable house. Hudson sold it on 20 years later and in 1944, the merchant banker, Sir Edward de Stein gave it to the National Trust.

Paths pass either side of the castle mound, although the entrance lies on the seaward flank. Beyond, a track leads around the harbour bay towards the village. Fork left at a junction **C**, passing a collection of upturned boats that serve as fishermen's sheds. Approaching the jetty area, bear right in front of a large hut to find a path climbing onto the Heugh behind, which overlooks the priory and offshore island to which St Cuthbert retreated before withdrawing to Inner Farne.

The path drops steeply from the far end, where a track curves up right past St Mary's Church. Turn in through the churchyard and leave by the northern gate past the Priory Museum. The present ruins date from its refoundation as a Benedictine house in the 11th century, when monks returned from Durham. The small community briefly prospered, but the surrounding area was repeatedly harried during border unrest before its dissolution in 1537.

Now carry on and walk into the village centre keeping ahead at the crossroads **D** in order to return to the car park. ●

Coldingham Bay and St Abb's Head

		GPS waypoints
Start	Coldingham Bay, ¾ mile east of Coldingham village	▨ NT 915 665
Distance	5¾ miles (9.3km)	Ⓐ NT 919 672
Height gain	1,015 feet (310m)	Ⓑ NT 916 674
		Ⓒ NT 913 691
Approximate time	3 hours	Ⓓ NT 908 689
		Ⓔ NT 913 685
Parking	Car park at start	Ⓕ NT 912 673
Route terrain	Clear paths and tracks, cliff edge	Ⓖ NT 913 667
Ordnance Survey maps	Landranger 67 (Duns, Dunbar & Eyemouth), Explorer 346 (Berwick-upon-Tweed)	

St Abb's Head is one of the spectacular sections of the eastern coastline, a progression of high sandstone cliffs twisting back from tiny coves and towering stacks. The popular beach at Coldingham and the headland nature reserve are both visited on this grand ramble above the cliffs, which returns via an inland loch and ancient path.

St Abbs takes its name from Æbbe, daughter of the Northumbrian king, Æthefrith, who founded a monastery following shipwreck in a storm upon this treacherous coast. The settlement was subsequently destroyed by an accidental fire, supposedly in retribution for 'disorderly' behaviour between the monks and nuns. The 12th-century priory at Coldingham was a Benedictine house for monks and suffered fluctuating fortunes until the Scottish Reformation in 1560 put a stop to monasticism. The church continued in use by the parish, although was badly damaged when Cromwell passed by in 1650.

▨ Walk past **St Vedas Hotel** and keep right to the beach, where, in the best seaside tradition, there is a motley line of bathing huts. Turn left along the head of the beach towards a gnarled stack rising above the rocks at the far

end of the shore. However, before that point, a flight of steps takes the route up to join a tarmac path along the cliff top to St Abbs. Reaching a signpost, turn left along a street lined by low cottages, Murrayfield.

Go right at the T-junction Ⓐ and then swing left with the main street as it curves high above the harbour. Keep left again at the far end, passing the church where you can abandon the tarmac for a parallel footpath on the left. When it finishes, cross to a path opposite Ⓑ, which is signed to St Abb's Head and runs away beside a high stone wall.

Regaining the coast, climb above Starney Bay past a succession of inaccessible coves and sea-washed rocks before dropping to the head of Horsecastle Bay. Turning from the sea, follow the foot of Kirk Hill, part of which is a protected habitat for the northern brown argus butterfly.

Beyond, the path gains height towards the coast, giving sight of the sea once more. The lighthouse also comes into view, set upon a squat building partway down a spit in order to shine below the fog that often obscures the cliff tops. Pass left of the lighthouse cottages and drop to a metalled drive **C**. However, first you might climb left to a hilltop viewpoint for a magnificent panorama that sweeps inland across the Cheviot and Border hills.

Instead of simply following the lane, take a convoluted path above the dramatic cliffs, but *be wary of the precipice*. Thousands of seabirds nest here in late spring; guillemots and razorbills crowding narrow ledges on the stacks, while kittiwakes and fulmars build nests on the sheer cliff. A handful of puffins hide their eggs in tiny crevices, while on the slabs below you will see shags and herring gulls.

The path winds back to join the lane as it drops steeply through a hairpin to the head of a small bay. Climb away, but leave just before a cattle-grid **D**, following a trod over a stile in an intervening fence and past a reed bed at the head of Mire Loch. The way weaves through scrub above the western bank, meeting a track at the far end **E**. Head uphill to rejoin the lighthouse lane, which wanders on for some ¾ mile to Northfield Farm.

Approaching the main lane, turn back left **F** to a car park, taking a path at the far side past the information centre and **seasonal café**. Carry on along the road, which as before can be avoided by parallel paths on the left and then the right. Retrace your steps above

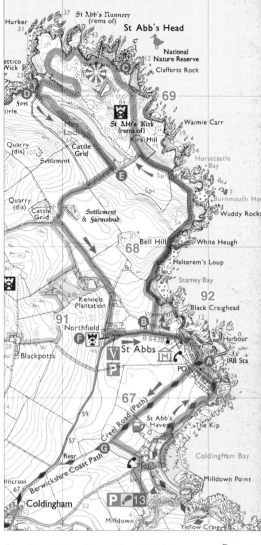

the harbour, turning right into Creel Road. This time, however, keep ahead to the end of the street and continue along a contained path. An ancient way, it was used by Coldingham's monks and fishermen to reach their boats moored below St Abbs. Becoming hedged, the path falls into a dip **G**, where a path is signed left to Coldingham Sands. Reaching a lane, turn right back to the start. ●

Melrose and the Eildon Hills

		GPS waypoints	
Start	Melrose		NT 547 339
Distance	5 miles (8km)	**A**	NT 547 337
Height gain	1,475 feet (450m)	**B**	NT 550 325
Approximate time	3 hours	**C**	NT 548 322
Parking	Melrose	**D**	NT 554 328
Route terrain	Generally good, but occasionally steep paths; a narrow wall-top path is avoidable	**E**	NT 563 336
		F	NT 561 341
Ordnance Survey maps	Landranger 73 (Peebles, Galashiels & Selkirk), Explorer 338 (Galashiels, Selkirk & Melrose)		

The striking landmarks of the three peaks of the Eildon Hills all offer stunning views from their summits. This walk takes in the two highest, returning in a roundabout route beside the River Tweed. Although fairly short, the climb onto middle peak is quite steep, as is the descent from northern hill. The final stretch by the river runs along the top of a narrow wall, but there is an alternative finish.

Aidan, the Ionian missionary who brought Christianity to Northumbria, founded the first monastery at Melrose in 660. Cuthbert began his vocation here and became its second prior, and

Melrose Abbey

Melrose is traditionally one of the places where the Lindisfarne monks laid his body during their wandering search for a new home. The present ruins are of a Cistercian foundation under David I in 1131, the town growing to serve both the needs of the monks and pilgrims visiting the abbey church. Like other border towns, Melrose periodically suffered from the attacks and reprisals of both sides, the abbey finally being destroyed around 1550. Sir Walter Scott and the Duke of Buccleuch were responsible for its restoration in 1822.

Begin from the Market Cross in the Square, leaving south along Dingleton Road, which climbs away beneath the bypass. Some 100 yds beyond the bridge, look for a stepped path signed as the Eildon Hills Walk and St Cuthbert's Way **A**, which drops between the terraces to a bridge over Malthouse Burn.

The onward path rises left behind the cottages before turning up a long flight of steps beside a wood. Over a stile, the way continues energetically upwards, offering an excuse to pause and admire the retrospective view over the town and its abbey. Through a couple of gates, cross the end of a track and resume the steep ascent. Emerging through a kissing-gate onto the open hillside, walk up to a waymark and bear right. The path winds through gorse to a shallow saddle between the northern and middle hills **B**, where a superb view suddenly opens to the south.

Tackle Mid Hill first, taking the rising path to the right and keeping right where it shortly forks. Higher up, the gradient briefly eases before the path swings left in a final determined attack of the summit cone **C**. The panorama from the top is quite magnificent, a topograph helping you to identify the surrounding hills. On a shelf, just below

0	200	400	600	800 METRES	1	KILOMETRES
						MILES
0	200	400	600 YARDS		1/2	

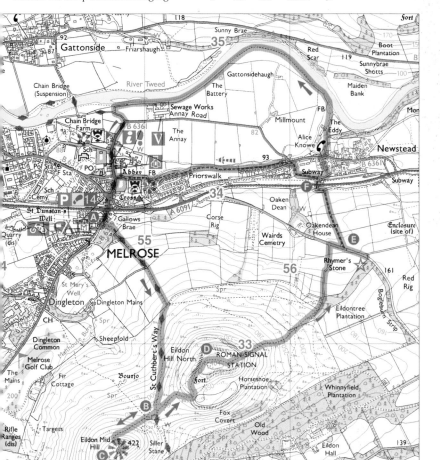

Eildon Hill North

to the right is a burial cairn, while to the south is the lowest hill of the group.

Return to the saddle and continue onto the northern hill. The climb is less strenuous and although all upward paths will take you to the top, the broadest trail takes the easiest line to a low pile of stones marking the summit **D**.

Carry on along a short grassy ridge, at the end of which bear left on a path descending through the heather and blaeberry. The way progressively steepens to a waymark. Continue straight down the hill to another waymark and again keep ahead between patches of gorse. Meeting a junction of paths before a line of beech masking a plantation of pine, go left, shortly passing through a gate. An old hedged path runs down to meet a lane, formerly the main road into the town.

Go right, passing through a barrier to find a stone stele 100 yds farther on. 'This stone marks the site of the Eildon Tree, where legend says Thomas the Rhymer met the Queen of the Fairies and here he was inspired to utter the first notes of the Scottish Muse'. The original site lay somewhat to the south, but the stone was relocated in 1970.

Return through the barrier and take the track just beyond on the right **E**, which falls between the fields. At the bottom, go through the right-hand gate, winding through an underpass below the A6091. Continue beneath an old railway bridge to a T-junction of tracks **F**.

Those not comfortable with heights should turn left and follow Eildon Hills Walk waymarks back to the town. Otherwise, go right to a cottage and then turn left down Claymires Lane. Coming out onto a street at the bottom walk right and then almost immediately left into Eddy Road. It soon degrades to a rough track, from the end of which a trod continues over a footbridge to the Tweed.

Turn upstream over a stile and along a walkway to carry on by the river at the edge of a large grazing meadow. Reaching the far side, the route climbs onto a high stone wall known as Battery Dyke. It runs above the river for ¼ mile, dropping off at the end to continue past a water treatment plant and rugby ground. Passing through a metal gate go left at the edge of a small field to emerge through another gate onto a lane. Turn left again past the rugby ground to a junction. Go right to pass the abbey and Priorwood Garden and keep ahead back to the centre of Melrose. ●

Bolam Lake and Shaftoe Crags

		GPS waypoints
Start	Bolam Lake Country Park	NZ 083 820
Distance	6½ miles (10.5km)	Ⓐ NZ 074 819
Height gain	540 feet (165m)	Ⓑ NZ 073 813
Approximate time	3 hours	Ⓒ NZ 060 805
Parking	Boathouse Wood car park (Pay and Display)	Ⓓ NZ 059 817
		Ⓔ NZ 051 824
Route terrain	Clear paths, tracks and lane	Ⓕ NZ 076 818
Ordnance Survey maps	Landranger 81 (Alnwick & Morpeth), Explorer OL42 (Kielder Water & Forest)	

A circuit around Bolam Lake makes a fine, easy walk on its own, but here, the country park serves as a base from which to explore the wider countryside. Nearby are the impressive sandstone and heath outcrops of Shaftoe Crags, a superb viewpoint across the rolling landscape towards Wallington.

The woodland lake was laid out in the early 19th century and provided timber during the last war. Restoration as a country park has created many habitats for wildlife, which include red squirrels,

weasels, stoats and of course the lake's resident mute swans.

From the car park, drop to the lake and follow the shore path in a clockwise direction. Reaching a fork, bear right past the car park at Lower House Wood and keep going to West

Bolam Lake

Wood car park. From the far side, amble on through the trees parallel to the lane. Ignore a broad grass trail and continue to the corner of the wood, emerging at a junction Ⓐ.

Take the narrow lane opposite signed to Harnham, which, after passing through a belt of trees, soon crosses a cattle-grid onto the edge of open grazing. Shaftoe Crags can be seen in the middle distance to the right. After nearly ½ mile, cross a stream and go right at the junction beyond, Ⓑ. The way lies along a shallow fold past Sandyford Farm and below Toft Hill, its slopes ridged with old ploughing. Keep going for almost a mile, passing a lone cottage before reaching a path signed off on the right Ⓒ. It traces the margin dividing open cultivation towards East Shaftoe Hall. Over a stile and bridge, the path crosses the line of a Roman road, the Devil's Causeway, which ran from Corbridge to the coast at Berwick. Carry on to a track in front of the farm Ⓓ and follow it left above a walled garden and then past a cottage to a gate.

The old track winds away across open heath, rising gently onto the hillside.

Salters Nick

The mound of high ground to the left was the site of an Iron Age settlement, its embankments and ditches still visible among the bracken. Above the track to the right is the highpoint of the

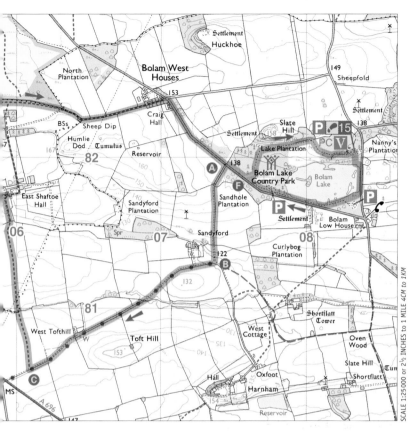

hill, marked by a triangulation pillar, from which there is a wonderful view across the surrounding countryside.

Return to continue along the main track, which curves around the flank of the hill to Shaftoe Grange. Approaching the house, bear right to pass it and walk on at the edge of the heath below a line of weatherworn cliffs. In a rock shelter, flints dating from the early Stone Age have been found, while some rocks bear cup-shaped carvings from the Bronze Age.

Carry on for ¼ mile to the corner of the accompanying wall **E**, there swinging right on a track that rises to a gap in the sandstone outcrop, Salters Nick. Another Iron Age settlement, which continued into the Roman period, was sited on the high ground here. The dramatic scenery is suddenly left

behind, the bridlepath passing from the heath onto open grazing. As a track joins from the right, walk on through a gate, shortly beyond which the distinctive mound of a Bronze Age burial tumulus can be seen to the right. The track ends past the cottages at Bolam West Houses at a lane.

Turn right towards Belsay and Newcastle, walking for a little over ¼ mile back to the junction for Harnham **A**. Retrace your outward path into the woods, but on reaching the green trail **F** just before West Wood car park, go left. Winding through the trees, it is shortly joined by another path from the left. Keep going as the trees then thin to reveal the lake below. Remain on the high path, which shortly passes into more woodland, later bearing right at a fork to return to the car park. ●

Hadrian's Wall from Once Brewed

Hadrian's Wall from Once Brewed

Start	Once Brewed
Distance	6¾ miles (10.9km)
Height gain	900 feet (275m)
Approximate time	3 hours
Parking	National Park car park (Pay and Display)
Route terrain	Rugged field and moorland paths
Ordnance Survey maps	Landranger 86 (Haltwhistle & Brampton) or 87 (Hexham & Haltwhistle), Explorer OL43 (Hadrian's Wall – Haltwhistle & Hexham)

GPS waypoints

- 🗒 NY 752 668
- Ⓐ NY 748 668
- Ⓑ NY 740 655
- Ⓒ NY 730 656
- Ⓓ NY 714 657
- Ⓔ NY 715 662
- Ⓕ NY 727 668
- Ⓖ NY 750 675

Hadrian's Wall is at its most impressive across the Pennines, its formidability heightened by the line of crags upon which it sits. Beginning from the Once Brewed Visitor Centre, the walk climbs to the Stanegate, a military road servicing the frontier defence. The route then loops west to Cawfield Crags and follows the wall for some 2½ miles, passing its highest elevation on Winshield Crags.

🗒 Walk up to the main road and turn left past the famous **Twice Brewed Inn**. The origin of its name is lost in time, but a couple of tales play on the quality of its ale. Edward I, on his way to Berwick, was so pleased with his pint that he commanded it be brewed again. But General Wade's men, passing by in pursuit of Bonnie Prince Charlie, were not impressed and ordered it to be brewed again. It all goes to show what a change of landlord can do, but

what of 'Once Brewed'? When Lady Trevelyan of Wallington Hall, whose husband was a strict abstainer, opened the youth hostel in 1934, she declared that nothing stronger than tea would be served and hoped that even that 'would only be brewed once'.

After ¼ mile, just before the Vallum Lodge guesthouse, turn off left along a signed path beside a small workshed **Ⓐ**. Walk away at the field edge and cross a stream at the bottom. Bearing right, climb past a ruin and over a stile in an intervening fence towards a roofless barn on the skyline.

Through a gate beside it, cross the line of the Stanegate, the raised way and parallel ditches clearly evident in the tussock. Strike a right diagonal across an expanse of rough pasture to find a ladder-stile in the distant corner opposite Bayldon Farm **Ⓑ**. Follow a grass track to the right to meet the bend

in a lane. Again go right, leaving on the next bend through a gate on the left from which a path is signed to Haltwhistle **Ⓒ**.

Walk below a rocky ridge, continuing past the corner of the wall to find a small gate and stile in a wall on the far side of a hollow. Head away on a trod, crossing a stream towards a clump of trees. Rising from a second dip, the path curves left, becoming more distinct to follow a line of shallow sinks. Emerging over a stile onto a lane **Ⓓ**, follow it downhill to the main road beside the **Milecastle Inn**.

The lane opposite heads toward Cawfield Crags, passing mounds in the adjacent field that mark the site of a Roman fort. Leave through a kissing-gate on the bend **Ⓔ** and strike out,

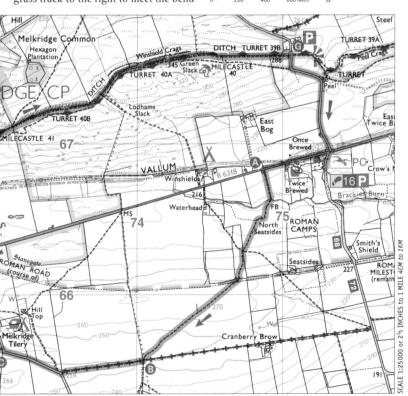

Milecastle 42 from the top of Cawfield Crags

crossing the line of the vallum before climbing to a milecastle at the end of the crag. The square ruin is immediately impressive, but an even better view is to be had by clambering up the fenced path to the top of the stark cliff. The cliff and lake below are not natural features but an abandoned quarry, opened during the 19th century to exploit the outcrop of hard, whinstone, but taking with it a section of Roman wall.

The onward way follows the heaving ridge to the right, where the ancient defensive wall has been restored to an impressive shoulder height. Steps take the path onto another prominence, Thorny Doors, after which the way becomes more rugged towards Caw Gap Turret. Drop to cross a lane **F** and

continue on a path signed to Steel Rigg and Housesteads. Here, only a dry-stone field boundary marks the wall, undulating steadily upwards to the high point on Winshield Crags. The eye-filling panorama takes in the line of the Roman wall across its most desolate section. In the distant west is the Solway Firth and to the north, the Cheviot Hills. Closer to, the shallow marshy valley below the wall harbours a series of loughs, the largest of which, Greenlee Lough is a nature reserve.

As you continue east, the ground steadily falls, the path shortly coming out once again onto a lane **G**. Follow it right down the hill back to the main road opposite Once Brewed. ●

St Cuthbert's Cave

		GPS waypoints
Start	Holburn Grange	NU 051 351
Distance	7 miles (11.3km)	(A) NU 054 354
Height gain	785 feet (240m)	(B) NU 059 352
Approximate time	3½ hours	(C) NU 069 341
Parking	Car park behind the grange (signed to St Cuthbert's Cave from the main lane)	(D) NU 083 350
		(E) NU 067 358
		(F) NU 060 352
Route terrain	Generally clear paths and tracks	(G) NU 045 361
Ordnance Survey maps	Landranger 75 (Berwick-upon-Tweed), Explorer 340 (Holy Island and Bamburgh)	

Set back from the Northumberland coast is a low range of sandstone hills, culminating in heughs and craggy outcrops that offer fabulous views to Holy Island and the Farne Islands, while to the south west are the distant Cheviots. One of the most dramatic viewpoints is Greensheen Hill, featured on this superb walk from Holburn Grange, which also passes a striking rock shelter, one of the traditional places where the monks, carrying the sacred remains of St Cuthbert, rested during their long, wandering journey.

A hedged grass track rises from beside the car park towards Greensheen Hill. Over a stile at the top (A), go right on a green track contouring the heath of the higher slopes. Mounting another stile, walk within a fringe of a pine woodland. After a few yards, bear off along a narrow path into the trees, which leads to the foot of St Cuthbert's Cave (B).

After St Cuthbert died in 687 on Inner Farne, his body was taken for interment at Lindisfarne. His tomb became a place of pilgrimage as tales of miracles spread. But the monastery was repeatedly harassed by Viking raiders and, in 875, they were eventually forced to leave in search of a safe haven, taking with them their most treasured possession, the miraculously still-

preserved body of St Cuthbert. For seven troubled years, the brothers roamed northern England before settling at Chester-le-Street. However, renewed raids in the 10th century again displaced the community and the monks removed the saint to Ripon. When things later quietened down, they set off back for Chester-le-Street, but while resting at Durham, the corpse let it be known that this was where he wanted to stay. A stone church was built to house his tomb, but that was not quite the end, for he was moved yet again when the cathedral was built in 1104.

A broader track returns you to the main path. Continue left, exchanging the pine for larch, where a clearing reveals weatherworn outcrops of sandstone standing below more impressive cliffs. Keep going as the track bends into the thick of the forest, losing the views to the Cheviot Hills. Ignore a track leaving right at the crest of the hill and curve around to a gate leading out of the trees **C**.

As the path falls at the edge of open grazing, the panorama is towards the sea and the low offshore rocks of the Farne Islands. Through another patch of woodland, walk past a couple of sturdy barns to join an enclosed track that descends almost dead straight for the next ½ mile.

Reaching a junction beside a barn at Swinhoe Farm **D**, turn left, the way signed to Holburn. Approaching more timber, disregard tracks off to the right and wind past Swinhoe lakes. After gently climbing, the winding track finally leaves the trees. Stride on below a low gorse-covered heugh, eventually reaching a gate and junction **E**.

Ignore the gate and instead, turn

sharp left on a diagonal course out of the corner, a fingerpost pointing the way to St Cuthbert's Cave. Over a low rise, descend to a gate and head straight across to a gated bridge at the foot of

St Cuthbert's Cave

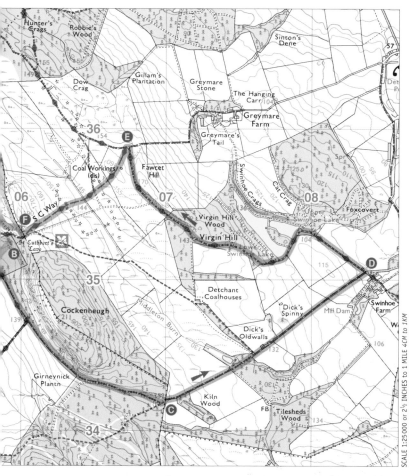

SCALE 1:25 000 or 2½ INCHES to 1 MILE 4CM to 1KM

the next rough pasture. Maintain direction up the rising hillside, aiming for the right-hand forest edge on the skyline. At the crest, walk into the corner where fence and wall meet, there passing through a couple of gates **F**.

A narrow path follows the western side of the wall right to a ladder-stile, over which, you can climb to the top of the adjacent outcrop for a grand view back to the coast. Return across the ladder-stile and continue along the heathery path, which snakes to the survey pillar on the summit of Greensheen Hill.

Having satiated yourself with the view, wander on, gently losing height along the ridge towards Holburn Moss.

The broadening path swings left before Holburn Lake, closing with a wall and following it to a gate. Carry on downhill on the other side of the wall to join a track. Where that then swings towards the farm, leave through a field gate on the left **G**.

A trod shows the way at the edge of rough grazing, shortly winding with the fence to settle as a more prominent path along the bracken and gorse fringe below Greensheen Hill. After ½ mile it brings you to the top of the track above Holburn Grange **A**, which leads back to the car park. ●

Peebles and the River Tweed

		GPS waypoints	
Start	Peebles	🖉	NT 249 403
Distance	7¼ miles (11.7km)	Ⓐ	NT 232 401
Height gain	560 feet (170m)	Ⓑ	NT 228 395
Approximate time	3 hours	Ⓒ	NT 209 399
Parking	Swimming pool car park (Pay and Display)	Ⓓ	NT 206 397
		Ⓔ	NT 217 388
Route terrain	Clear paths and tracks	Ⓕ	NT 230 393
		Ⓖ	NT 244 401
Ordnance Survey maps	Landranger 73 (Peebles, Galashiels & Selkirk), Explorer 337 (Peebles & Innerleithen)		

Hardly anywhere along the length of the River Tweed is its course less than attractive, but the stretch above the ancient border town of Peebles is particularly fine. This circuit begins along the northern bank below the striking Neidpath Castle, generally following the course of an old railway to Lyne Bridge. There is a flavour of the surrounding countryside too, as the route climbs to the superb viewpoint at Manor Sware on its meandering return to the town.

A favourite residence of the kings of Scotland, Peebles was a royal burgh by the time of King David I. Although escaping much of the Border conflict, it was razed by the British in 1549 and suffered again a century later when occupied by Cromwell's troops. Despite poverty during the 18th century, the railway age brought better times and it gained a reputation as a fashionable spa with the opening of the Peebles Hydro in 1881. An attractive town, it has no shortage of fine eating places and is a popular centre for walkers, anglers and

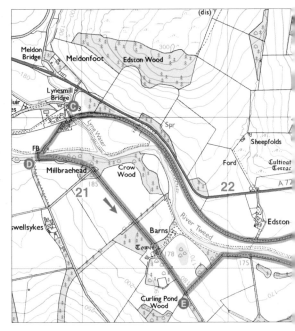

golfers. One of the high spots of its calendar is the Beltane Festival, a colourful week of events held each June that has its origins in a Celtic celebration marking the return of the summer.

🖊 Leave the far end of the swimming pool car park along a riverside path, crossing a bridge spanning Eddlestone Water. Climb steps and go left behind houses, dropping beyond to Hay Lodge Park. Passing a footbridge, continue through the park, beyond which a more rugged path winds into a narrowing valley. Overlooking a clearing, Neidpath Castle was built in the 14th century by Sir William Hay, the Sheriff of Peebles on the site of an earlier castle. After changing allegiances, his descendant John Hay sided with Charles and, according to some, the castle surrendered only after a damaging siege by Cromwell's forces. Although later modernised, the castle fell into neglect and the romantic ruin inspired Sir Walter Scott to pen a poem about its ghost, *the Maid of Neidpath.*

The valley sides once more draw in, forcing the onward path into undulations along the steep wooded bank. Pretty views open through the trees, which soon stand back to reveal the Neidpath Viaduct. It carried a picturesque branch line between Symington and Peebles, which opened in 1860. After crossing the viaduct, the line disappeared into a tunnel for the final stretch into Peebles.

Through a gate beneath the bridge Ⓐ, mount the embankment and walk away along the trackbed. Emerging from a gentle curve the line runs dead straight above riverside meadows, the trees thinning to give a memorable view to the hills. After ½ mile, a missing bridge forces you off the embankment to cross a lane Ⓑ. *To the left, Manor Bridge offers a shortcut to the return route.* The main route, however, climbs back onto the embankment opposite,

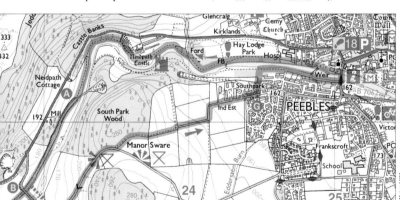

Approaching Peebles

following it for 1½ miles to a bridge over Lyne Water **C**. Drop to the narrow lane below and go right. Soon degrading to a track, it leads to a footbridge across the River Tweed **D**.

The path swings downstream along a woodland strip above the river, before long joining a broader path that leads to a cottage at Millbraehead. Keep ahead along a private track onto the Wemyss and March Estate. Signed as the Tweed Walk, it is a lovely avenue of stately old lime trees, which runs dead-straight between the fields and eventually leads to a junction overlooked by a 15th-century tower house, Barns Tower. Again go forward, passing the stables and as you continue along the track, look back left to see the later mansion, built in the 18th century once peace had settled on the troubled border.

After another ¼ mile, the Tweed Walk is directed off over a stile on the left **E**. A green track across the fields takes you back to the riverbank. Continue downstream beside the meadows on a tree-lined path to Manor Bridge.

Join the lane and walk away from the bridge, soon bearing left at a fork **F** down to Old Manor Bridge, a graceful,

single arch of stone built in 1702. Beyond, a narrow lane, now closed to traffic, rises steadily uphill, passing a viewpoint towards the top from which there is a stunning retrospective vista along the valley.

Carry on around the bend to find a gate on the left into South Park Wood, from which a path is signed to Peebles. Where it then divides, branch right within the fringe of the wood. Reaching the corner, leave over a stile and head down at the perimeter of grazing. A view opens to the town below, the towers and steeples of its churches standing prominent above the other buildings. From a gate at the bottom corner, a broad, fenced path winds down, emerging in South Parks on the outskirts of Peebles. Walk ahead, but just beyond Edderston Ridge, take a tarmac path on the left **G**. At the bottom of steps, keep ahead to regain the riverbank and turn right, picking up a waterside path back to the town. Climb out to the main road and turn over the bridge back to the swimming baths and car park. ●

Kelso, Roxburgh and the River Teviot

		GPS waypoints
Start	Kelso	
Distance	7½ miles (12.1km)	📝 NT 727 339
Height gain	510 feet (155m)	Ⓐ NT 727 335
		Ⓑ NT 723 327
Approximate time	3½ hours	Ⓒ NT 703 304
Parking	Kelso	Ⓓ NT 697 305
		Ⓔ NT 703 313
Route terrain	Clear paths; *Note: the riverside return may be flooded following exceptional rain*	Ⓕ NT 719 336
Ordnance Survey maps	Landranger 74 (Kelso & Coldstream), Explorer 339 (Kelso, Coldstream & Lower Tweed Valley)	

Exploring the Teviot Valley upstream of its confluence with the River Tweed, this walk begins from the ancient abbey town of Kelso. It follows the course of a disused railway to an impressive viaduct above the present day village of Roxburgh before returning along the riverbank past the once-grand castle upon which the historical royal burgh of Roxburgh was centred.

Kelso grew around the abbey, founded by King David I in 1128. Despite centuries of border raids, it became the wealthiest monastery in Scotland until the English largely destroyed its fabric in 1547. Following the Reformation in 1560, it fell derelict, much of its stone being pillaged for reuse in the town's buildings.

📝 With your back to the town hall, cross the impressive cobbled square and turn left into Bridge Street. Walk past the abbey ruins and over the Tweed on John Rennie's elegant bridge before dropping left into the park Ⓐ. Steps at the far corner regain the road beside the Millenium Viewpoint, which you should follow uphill. Swing sharp right at the junction along Jedburgh Road, soon leaving the town's houses behind.

Approaching the main road, cross to the entrance of Wallacenick Farm where there is a rough track off to the left Ⓑ, the course of the old railway. After ¼ mile, watch for a waymarked path forking off left, which winds beside a fence into a field. Follow the edge right, turning the corner to a small gate. Go right and left within the fringe of a small wood, leaving through a gate at the far corner. Bear left, climbing past the abutment of a bridge to rejoin the trackbed. The way meanders pleasantly along the hillside, affording a fine panorama across the valley. To the north, beyond the ruin of Roxburgh Castle is Floors Castle, while out west are the distinctive summits of the Eildon Hills.

Farther along, the track becomes increasingly wooded, eventually curving towards the Roxburgh Viaduct.

Kelso's five-arched bridge, designed by John Rennie in 1803

Although the route drops right at a waymark just before the viaduct **C**, it is worth continuing onto the bridge for the view. Return to the descending path, which leads to a narrow lane. At the foot of the viaduct, go right to find a footbridge, piggybacking the cutwaters across the river.

Following a sign for Lovers' Lane, cross ahead, but immediately bear right onto a contained path rising beside the embankment. At the top, there is a glimpse back through the hedge to the Wallace's Tower, the remains of a 16th-century tower house. The path ends at a junction beside the demolished bridges of Roxburgh Junction **D**.

Turn right through the village and carry on past Roxburgh Mill, where the lane briefly runs beside the river. As the lane bends away, leave over the second of two stiles on the right waymarked the Borders Abbeys Way **E**. Follow the field boundary right and then around the corner to continue above a low cliff overlooking the river, dropping at the end of the second field to a riverside

path. *Exceptionally, the river may flood its bank, in which case you must either retrace your route or follow the road back to Kelso.*

After a goodly mile, the path passes beneath the ruins of Roxburgh Castle, which can be accessed over a stile. The

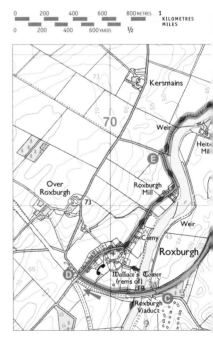

ancient royal burgh of Roxburgh lay within the protection of the castle on the spit of high land between the Teviot and Tweed rivers. It was taken several times by the English, in whose hands it remained from 1334 until 1460, when the castle was finally retaken by the Scots and demolished.

Beyond, the river curves sharply right, a flight of steps soon lifting the path from the bank. After passing behind a cottage, walk out to the main road **F** and follow it right over Teviot Bridge. Carry on to pass the confluence of the two rivers and turn back into Kelso. ●

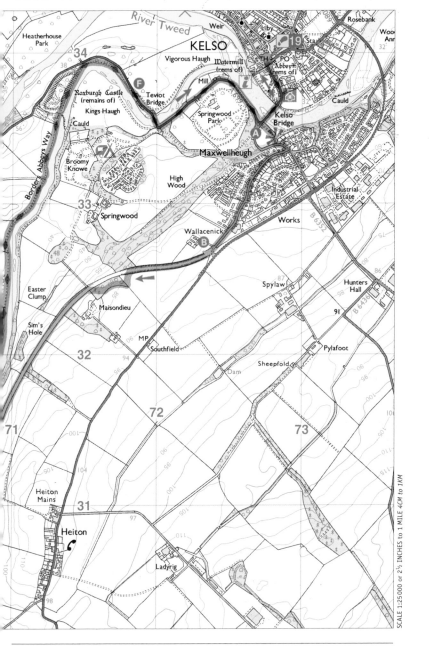

Craster, Howick and Longhoughton

		GPS waypoints
Start	Craster	 NU 256 198
Distance	8 miles (12.9km). Shorter version 5½ miles (8.9km)	**A** NU 261 174
		B NU 258 163
Height gain	605 feet (185m). Shorter version 475 feet (145m)	**C** NU 261 156
		D NU 242 158
Approximate time	3½ hours. Shorter version 2½ hours	**E** NU 250 175
		F NU 251 193
Parking	Car park at edge of village (Pay and Display)	
Route terrain	Clear paths, tracks and lanes	
Ordnance Survey maps	Landranger 81 (Alnwick & Morpeth), Explorer 332 (Alnwick & Amble)	

Most visitors to Craster are drawn along the coast to Dunstanburgh, completely ignoring the superb coastline that lies to the south. This longer, but undemanding walk follows the low cliffs past several inviting bays before turning inland to return across the fields. The final leg passes through a small nature reserve in the former quarries behind the village.

 Take the path from the car park towards Craster, swinging beyond its end along back streets to emerge opposite the **Jolly Fisherman**. Go left and then right beside it, turning through a rear gate into the beer garden. The coast path runs behind the houses, soon leaving the village to curve around a small cove, Hole 'o the Dike. It continues on springy turf above the sloping slabs and boulders of the shore.

Approaching Cullernose Point the rising path turns in above the impressive cliffs backing Swine Den. Passing through thicket, the way briefly closes with the lane before continuing along the cliff top towards the distinctive chimneys topping the isolated Bathing House, used by the Greys of Howick Hall when spending a day by the sea.

Just beyond the cottage, ignore the track swinging inland **A** and carry on past Rumbling Kern. The sheltered beach makes a great spot for a picnic, while the rock formations are full of interest and include a natural arch through which the incoming tide gushes.

Over a stile, the coast path continues behind the splendid beach at Howick Haven before then losing sight of the sea as it delves into bushes. A curious conical feature on top of the grass bank above is a reconstruction of a Mesolithic hut. It can be reached either

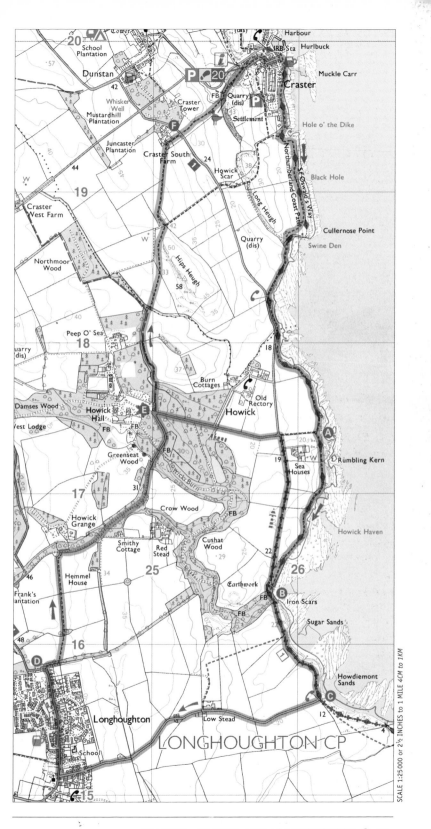

directly by scaling the steep slope to a stile or more easily, by doubling back along a farm track when you later emerge from the scrub above a small beach ⑧.

In the nearby fields overlooking Howick Burn are the embanked remains of an Iron Age camp. It was occupied, perhaps over a period of several hundred years prior to the Roman invasion of Britain from AD43. However, man first visited this part of the coast around 10,000 years ago and excavation has revealed traces of a Mesolithic settlement as well as later burials from the Bronze Age. The early Stone Age people followed a hunter-gather lifestyle in what were then coastal woodlands, catching small animals and birds and taking fish, shellfish and perhaps even seals from the sea. The reconstructed hut gives an idea of how such a family might have lived.

The track also serves as a short-cut bypassing Longhoughton village. Reaching the corner of a lane, go left to rejoin the main route at the entrance to Howick Hall ⑤.

Otherwise, cross the head of the cove to a bridge spanning Howick Burn and keep with the coast, where protruding rocky shelves separate a succession of sandy beaches. When you reach Howdiemont Sands ⓒ, turn away from the sea along a lane that passes through Low Stead Farm before eventually leading to Longhoughton. Emerging opposite the church, go right along the main street.

Where the road bends left at the far end of the village, leave on the corner ⑩ for a signed footpath that swings right to run within a belt of woodland. However, after only 150 yds, bear left through a gate opening and strike along the uncultivated margin between open fields. After passing through a wooded

dell, carry on at the edge of more fields, ultimately coming out onto a leafy lane. Turn right, in time dipping across Howick Burn and then passing beneath a bridge carrying one of the Howick estate drives to reach a sharp bend in front of the entrance to the hall and its gardens ⑤.

Although the origins of the present hall date from 1782, the Greys have held Howick since the 14th century. The most famous member of the family was Charles, the second Earl, who became Prime Minister in 1830. He is known for the 'Earl Grey' blend of tea, which was supposedly sent to him in gratitude by a Chinese Mandarin, whose son's life had been saved by one of Grey's envoys. The acclaimed gardens reflect an informal and natural style, which has been developed since 1920 and are only closed to visitors during the winter months.

Take the drive beside the lodge towards the car park, but where that then turns, keep ahead on a track that falls into a field. Walk on at the left edge above a wooded strip. Ignore a gate towards the far end of the second field, to find another in the corner. Through that, strike a diagonal across a crop field to a stile in the distant wall. Bear left below the gorse-blanketed outcrop of Hips Heugh, continuing to a gate beyond its end. Disregarding the crossing track keep going beside the right-hand boundary to Craster South Farm. Walk forward from the field behind a row of cottages and turn right out to a lane ⑥.

Through a kissing-gate opposite, a path heads across old meadows, ridged and furrowed from medieval ploughing. Leave through a gate at the bottom corner and walk back through the Arnold Nature Reserve to the car park. ●

Hadrian's Wall at Walltown and Thirlwall Castle

		GPS waypoints	
Start	Walltown Quarry, signed from Military Road (B6318), 1 mile east of Greenhead	✏	NY 668 659
		Ⓐ	NY 671 661
		Ⓑ	NY 704 667
Distance	7¾ miles (12.5km)	Ⓒ	NY 704 664
Height gain	1,020 feet (310m)	Ⓓ	NY 680 665
Approximate time	3½ hours	Ⓔ	NY 675 672
Parking	Car park at start (Pay and Display)	Ⓕ	NY 666 670
		Ⓖ	NY 663 670
Route terrain	Some rugged paths; Tipal Burn's stepping stones may occasionally be flooded	Ⓗ	NY 659 660
Ordnance Survey maps	Landranger 86 (Haltwhistle & Brampton), Explorer OL43 (Hadrian's Wall – Haltwhistle & Hexham)		

Those following Hadrian's Wall from the west get their first appreciation of its awesome scale at Walltown. Perversely, a century of quarrying the whin sill dolerite has added drama to the scene by creating an abrupt high cliff at the end of the crag. Exploring not only one of the most rugged sections of the wall, this walk takes in some of the countryside on both sides of the wall as well as visiting a medieval castle.

✏ Take the trail leaving the car park beside the toilet block. Immediately branch left above the lake and head towards the main quarry face. Climb to a kissing-gate and follow the boundary up to the Roman wall at the top of the rise Ⓐ.

Savour the stunning western view before continuing beside one of the best-preserved stretches of Hadrian's Wall.

Before long, the path drops steeply to a break in the cliffs, climbing equally determinedly to Turret 45a. There is some evidence that this pre-dated the wall and was incorporated within its structure. Progressing east, the route skirts another quarry face, rejoining the

An impressive limekiln near Walltown

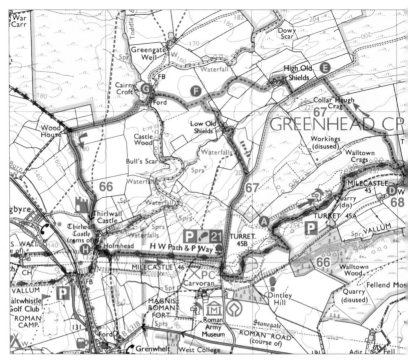

line of the wall beyond. After passing the scant outline of a milecastle, the path drops into a gap carrying a rough track through to the north. It is followed for the second part of the walk, but for the time being, cross the ladder-stile in front and climb steeply back onto the ridge, passing a turret, strategically sited to guard the gap.

Although only visible as a grassed mound of rubble along the cliff edge, the ongoing wall is no less dramatic. Carry on along the heaving ridge, later passing another milecastle, also robbed of its stone. The ground then gently falls to a small plantation, the path emerging at the far side by a farmstead, Cockmount Hill. Carry on at the field edge towards the next farm, Great Chesters, which stands behind a Roman infantry fort.

Although smaller and with fewer remains above ground than at Housesteads, the site is nevertheless impressive. Much of the perimeter wall

can be seen as well as the outlines of many of the buildings within the compound. Of particular interest, encircled by a fence, is a stone arch, part of the vaulting for an underground strong room, while the southern gateway is flanked by a well and a pedestal altar. As was usual, a civil settlement developed outside the fort, and here lay to the south west, where a cemetery was also discovered. To the south east was a bath house, an important focus of Roman social life. It drew its water from Caw Burn, some two miles to the north east, the water flowing along an aqueduct that snaked for six miles across the moss, crossing several other streams in the process.

Joining the farm track, leave the fort through its southern gateway **B**. Walk down to a narrow lane **C** and go right. Shortly degrading to a track, it follows the line of the vallum, a ditch flanked by earth ramparts that runs behind the wall throughout its length. It was

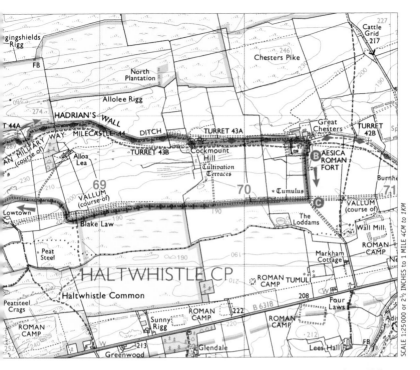

SCALE 1:25000 or 2½ INCHES to 1 MILE 4CM to 1KM

0	200	400	600	800 METRES	1	
						KILOMETRES
						MILES
0	200	400	600 YARDS	½		

constructed at some time after the wall and is now thought to have defined a military zone from which civilians were excluded. Later abandoning the vallum, the track eventually passes a limekiln by an old quarry and then winds to a junction, just before Walltown Farm . Beside it there are a pair of cattle troughs, the stone of which came from the Milecastle 45.

Turn right, climbing beneath King Arthur's Well, reputedly the spot where Paulinus baptised King Edwin prior to his marriage with Princess Ethelberga of Kent in 596. Cross the line of the wall and follow a rough stone track onto the moor. Pass through a gap in a field wall to cross a stream and, where the track then appears to fork, bear left. The path almost immediately disappears into tussock, but continue over the rise, aiming just right of High Old Shields, whose roof then appears in the middle distance, to find a ladder-stile across a wall. Walk down to a footbridge and the lane beyond **E**.

Go left, later turning in at the entrance to High Old Shields Farm. Crossing stiles at the top, pass right of the farmhouse into the field behind. Bear left behind cattle sheds to a stile and continue beside a wall before veering right to a stile in the bottom fence. Maintain the same line to a ladder-stile at the bottom. Go left, walking beyond the wall's end to cross another stile. Carry on to a signpost **F**.

Up to the left is Low Old Shields, the way back if the stepping stones across Tipal Burn are impassable. However, for the time being, keep ahead beside the ruin of a wall. As it peters out, curve right to pick up another line of rubble, which heads towards the white cottage and wind turbine of Cairny Croft on the far slope of the valley. The way drops to a stile above the riverbank, where to the left you will find stepping stones .

The footbridge marked on the map has long-since gone and if the crossing is flooded you must return to point **F** *and climb to Low Old Shields. There, wind through the farmyard and walk out along its access track. Reaching the lane, turn right back to the car park.*

Cross Tipal Burn to gain a lane below Cairny Croft and follow it left, winding uphill to a junction by Wood House. Keep left, shortly dropping to a sharp bend at the entrance to Thirlwall Castle. Bear left into the farm and then right, leaving through a gate to follow a track beside the castle.

First mention of the castle is of its fortification by the Thirlwalls during the 14th century, although it is said that Edward I slept here in 1306. The castle stood until the 1640s, when it was slighted after being taken by the Scots during the Civil War. The material for the castle's construction had come from the Roman wall, but its own ruination

was in turn hastened by the villagers scavenging stone for their cottages. Supposedly hidden beneath it is a table of solid gold, brought back from the Crusades together with its keeper, a hideous dwarf, by John de Thirlwall. News of his prize spread across the border, bringing down a band of murdering reivers. So the story goes, the dwarf saved himself and the table by jumping with it into the castle well, which promptly closed up behind him without trace, but his ghost still lingers, guarding the treasure.

Swing left past the castle entrance to a footbridge spanning Tipal Burn **H**. The ongoing track winds past Holmhead Cottage before rising to a gate. Climb steeply beside a deep ditch, continuing over a stile at the top. Without the impregnability afforded by the crags, a deep ditch ensured the security of the wall here. It survives the wall, which stood above it on the far side and remains a significant feature across the hillside. Emerging onto a lane, go right back to the car park. ●

Hadrian's Wall along Walltown Crags

Windy Gyle

		GPS waypoints	
Start	Rowhope Burn Bridge, ½ mile north west of Windyhaugh	🖉	NT 859 114
Distance	7¼ miles (11.7km)	**A**	NT 855 125
Height gain	1,640 feet (500m)	**B**	NT 859 147
		C	NT 855 152
Approximate time	4 hours	**D**	NT 835 149
Parking	Off-road parking beside bridge	**E**	NT 850 117
Route terrain	Reasonably clear, but remote moorland paths and tracks		
Ordnance Survey maps	Landranger 80 (Cheviot Hills & Kielder Water), Explorer OL16 (The Cheviot Hills)		

Deserted moors often beget forlorn-sounding names; The Slime and Foulstep Sike here conjuring particularly off-putting images. True, the area can be bleak, but catch it in the right mood and there is marvellous walking among a vast landscape of rolling hills, deep cleughs and long grassy ridges. One feature that does seem to live up to its name, however, is Windy Gyle, its top often kept clear of cobwebs by a lusty gale. The circuit is an extended horseshoe climbing above the catchments of Trows and Rowhope burns, which converge at Rowhope Farm to run into the main Coquet Valley. The paths are reasonably clear throughout, but inexperienced walkers are advised to save this trek for a clear day.

🖉 From the bridge at the foot of Rowhope Burn, take the tarmac side track signed to Rowhope and Uswayford. Carry on past Rowhope Farm to Trows Farm, just beyond which, the track meets a ford where two streams come together **A**. Cross the footbridge on the left spanning Trows Burn and follow a grass track through a gate to climb steadily along a broad grassy spur onto Trows Law. Higher up, through a second gate, the gradient eases to an enjoyable plod that opens expansive views on both sides. Although sometimes faint, the way sticks to the crest above the deepening

valley of Trows Burn. Ignore fragmenting trods off to the right and continue gaining height just east of north until, after 1½ miles, you meet an obvious crossing path at a waypost **B**.

Head left, now climbing towards the bulk of Windy Gyle. Shortly reaching another waymarked fork, branch right, the way soon levelling at a gate and stile. Beyond, a short flagged path leads to a trig point perched atop a sprawling heap of stones **C**.

The cairn is thought to date from the Bronze Age and is one of several along the ridge, which now forms the border between Scotland and England. Its

Looking into Scotland from Russell's Cairn

path is signed off left as The Street to the Coquet Valley. It soon passes through a gate to put the fence on your left, swapping views into Rowhope for those into neighbouring Carlcroft. Feral goats roam these hills and it is not unusual to see a small herd of these hardy animals. Through occasional gates, the way undulates easily onwards over Black Braes to skirt the shoulder of Swineside Law. Ignore paths forking right and keep with the fence as it later passes east of Bought Law. Eventually, 2½ miles of pleasant walking brings you to a gate by a waymark indicating a barely evident crossing bridleway **E**. Carry on ahead putting the fence now on your right, in time turning within the corner of the boundary. The way shortly begins to drop more steeply along the developing spur of the hill, the bridge at the foot of Rowhope Burn from which you started soon coming into view.

name refers to Lord Francis Russell, who attended one of the regular but fragile truces when the Wardens of the Marches met to bring those who had violated Border Law to justice. Trouble erupted when an Englishman refused to pay for spurs that he had bought from a Scottish pedlar and Lord Russell was killed in the ensuing affray. Coincidentally, his father, the second Earl of Bedford and a prominent politician, died of gangrene in London only hours later and the earldom passed over a generation to Francis's son, Edward.

Go left, following the Pennine Way off the top into a dip above the head of Rowhope Burn, the narrow saddle enabling grand views to the countries on either flank. Slip through a gate to climb away on the other side of the fence, ignoring a path off into Scotland towards the top. Carry on past the summit of an unnamed hill, but when the fence later bends away to the right, bear left, dropping across the head of Foulstep Sike. Rising beyond, there is a backward glance to the top of Windy Gyle before the path curves to a junction **D**.

Abandoning the Pennine Way, a good

The Street is one of several drove roads that crossed the border hills, along which cattle and sheep were herded into the Coquet Valley and on to English markets. The track was also used by itinerant traders who visited these remote communities on a regular round. Some of the lonely steadings doubled as inns, catering for these passing travellers. One such farmstead stood by the river here. Known as Slimefoot, it was a notorious haunt of smugglers carrying illicit whisky from stills hidden in the hills. Refreshment today can be got from the **Barrowburn Tea Room** at Windyhaugh. ●

Kirk Yetholm and the Halterburn Valley

		GPS waypoints
Start	Kirk Yetholm	🖉 NT 827 281
Distance	8½ miles (13.6km)	Ⓐ NT 839 276
Height gain	2,115 feet (645m)	Ⓑ NT 853 269
Approximate time	4½ hours	Ⓒ NT 858 235
Parking	Around the green at Kirk Yetholm	Ⓓ NT 846 256
Route terrain	Reasonably clear, but remote moorland paths and tracks	
Ordnance Survey maps	Landranger 74 (Kelso & Coldstream), Explorer OL16 (The Cheviot Hills)	

The 18th-century Border Hotel is a welcome sight for weary walkers completing the Pennine Way. This ramble combines the alternative routes of the trail's final leg, heading out on the long ridge from White Law to Black Hag and returning down the deep valley of Halter Burn. Although the paths are generally clear, inexperienced walkers should choose a clear day.

🖉 Signed as the Pennine and St Cuthbert's ways, High Street climbs from the village green over the shoulder of Staerough Hill into the Halter Burn Valley. At a cattle-grid Ⓐ, drop left to a footbridge spanning the stream and head up beside a wall. Just before the end, strike right across the bracken-clad flank of Green Humbleton. Curving from Shielknowe Burn, gain height to a fork where St Cuthbert's Way goes left. However, keep ahead with the Pennine

The border between Scotland and England below Whitelaw Nick

Cattle graze the slopes of Steerrig Knowe

Cheviot Hills. Through the gate, the path leaves the comforting guidance of the fence, bearing right past a waymark and dropping to a junction beside a signpost Ⓒ.

The Pennine Way low-level route is signed back right, falling above the source of Rowhope Burn to a gate. Beyond, the path loses height sharply above the headwaters of Curr Burn before passing through another gate into the upper reaches of the Halter Burn Valley.

The way now descends more easily towards Old Halterburnhead. Reaching the corner of a wall, follow it past the ruined steading, which huddles in the shelter of a clump of storm-ravaged trees.

Way, the path soon levelling onto Stob Rig and approaching a stone wall that marks the boundary between Scotland and England. Ignore the gate and stile into England Ⓑ and instead bear right beside the wall.

The path dips abruptly across the head of Witchcleuch Burn, rising sharply beyond to Whitelaw Nick. Cross a wall and bear left beside the frontier, ascending to the summit of White Law. At a junction of fences there, ignore the gate and swing right with the ongoing boundary. As the path falls once more there is a view ahead to The Cheviot.

Beyond a saddle, the way progresses steadily along Steer Rig. Approaching the final ascent onto Steerrig Knowe, a prominent ditch and embankment crossing the path marks an ancient boundary. After another gate the gradient eases, shortly arriving at a junction of fences and wall. This is the highest point of the walk and affords a grand panorama across the northern

Just beyond, the Pennine Way swings left, continuing down the valley to Burnhead. Approaching the farm, watch for a sign Ⓓ indicating a trod on the right that winds down to a sturdy wooden bridge spanning the stream. Go left to a kissing-gate and accompany the wall above the farm. Over a stile beside a gate, walk out to a track and follow it down the valley. Shortly after passing the cottages of Halterburn, pick up your outward route at the cattle-grid Ⓐ to return over the hill to Kirk Yetholm.

The 268-mile Pennine Way was the first long distance national trail to be established in the country and was opened in 1965. Conceived by Tom Stephenson 30 years earlier, it rambles across some of the wildest landscape in the Pennines between Edale in Derbyshire and Kirk Yetholm, just inside the Scottish border. ⬤

Cauldshiels Loch and the River Tweed

		GPS waypoints	
Start	Gun Knowe Loch, Tweedbank (on the eastern outskirts of Galashiels)	**GPS waypoints**	
		✐	NT 517 346
		Ⓐ	NT 510 343
Distance	10 miles (16.1km)	Ⓑ	NT 510 330
Height gain	1,150 feet (350m)	Ⓒ	NT 509 324
Approximate time	4½ hours	Ⓓ	NT 502 299
		Ⓔ	NT 488 322
Parking	Car park at start	Ⓕ	NT 513 353
Route terrain	Lanes and clear paths		
Ordnance Survey maps	Landranger 73 (Peebles, Galashiels & Selkirk), Explorer 338 (Galashiels, Selkirk & Melrose)		

After a brief dalliance with the Tweed from a park at the edge of Galashiels, the route climbs from Abbotsford along forgotten country lanes to Cauldshiels Loch, a serene beauty spot tucked in the hills. An enjoyable saunter across upland grazing precedes an easy descent and return beside the river, a picturesque stretch much frequented by fishermen.

Previously a marsh where the townspeople would come to skate in winter, Gun Knowe Loch was created in 1978 and now attracts a wide range of waterbirds, including the seemingly resident mute swans.

✐ From the car park follow the lakeside path in a clockwise direction. At the second junction, bear left, continuing past a football pitch toward trees at the far corner of the park. Picking up Borders Abbeys Way signs, pass behind houses along a steep wooded bank above the Tweed. Just before the main road, take a stepped path that dips beneath the bypass. Descend beyond into the wood, joining a broader track at the bottom. Climb to the B6360, emerging near the entrance to Abbotsford Ⓐ.

Abbotsford was the home of Sir Walter Scott, who became Scotland's greatest writer and father of the historical novel, *Rob Roy*, *Ivanhoe* and *Kenilworth* being among his best-known. He commissioned the splendid house in 1817 and lived there until his death in 1832.

Cross to a narrow lane opposite, which rises through a verdant tunnel. Bending left in front of a cattle shed, carry on to a junction. Go right gaining more height, which opens a view towards the Eildon Hills. Wind past the picturesque pool at Abbotsmoss and, at the end, turn right again. Walk up the lane for ¼ mile to reach a small parking area beside a crossing track Ⓑ, where Cauldshiels Loch is signed to the left. Climb towards a forest plantation and swing within a fringe of ancient gnarled beech. Carry on beyond the track's end to the loch shore, a delightful spot for a picnic.

The onward path follows the shore to the right, soon meeting a broader path. Go right to a track **C** and turn left, climbing past more majestic beech trees over the shoulder of Dod. Out to the left is Cauldshiels Hill, its top crowned by an ancient defensive earthwork.

Swinging left by a corrugated barn, go through a couple of gates and continue beside a wall across upland grazing. Gently climbing, the way curves towards the transmitter mast on Lindean Moor, revealing views across the confluence of the Tweed and Ettrick valleys to the higher hills. Over the crest the path descends past another beech-fringed plantation, finally leaving the pastures along a short, rough track up to a lane **D**.

Falling steadily downhill, the quiet lane offers 1½ miles of easy walking, eventually ending at a junction with the A7. Cross to the minor lane opposite, which winds over a bridge spanning Ettrick Water. Formerly the main road, it runs beside the park of Sunderland Hall, across which there is a brief view of the elegant 18th-century mansion. Bending at the far end, the lane turns over a second bridge, this time crossing the River Tweed.

Immediately over the bridge, and just in front of a cycle track, go through a gate on the right **E** from which steps drop to the riverbank. A trod tacks the field edge past the confluence with Ettrick Water and beneath the modern road bridge. Before long, a track develops, which then moves from the river behind a small plantation to join the course of an old branch line that ran from Galashiels to Selkirk. Opened in 1856, it served the woollen mills for which the town was famous.

Walk on to meet a narrow lane that leads past the few houses at Boleside and then beside a small park, where you

SCALE 1:27777 or 2¼ INCHES to 1 MILE 3.6CM to 1KM

can rejoin the river. Later forced to return to the lane, carry on past a fork, just beyond which, a sign marks the Southern Upland Way branching back to the Tweed. Paralleling the lane, the way undulates through the trees, giving a glimpse to Abbotsford on the opposite bank.

Eventually the way passes beneath a high bridge carrying the main road. Remain by the river past a car park and then at the edge of a field until forced away by a tributary stream, Gala Water. Follow that up to a road and go right over a bridge. Walk to the top of a rise, there taking a path on the right **F**, which crosses the Tweed on a viaduct built for the Waverley Line, which linked Edinburgh with Carlisle. Immediately over, drop to the right and walk from the bridge. Fork right beside a small substation to regain the riverbank, where, despite the proximity of the town, you might see an otter. After some 250 yds, leave the Tweed, turning towards a park. Keep ahead across the open playing fields, finally returning to Gun Knowe Loch. You can skirt around it either left or right back to the car park.

Hartside, Salter's Road and High Cantle

		GPS waypoints
Start	Hartside, 6 miles west of A697, beyond Powburn and Ingram	🖉 NT 976 161
Distance	8½ miles (13.7km)	Ⓐ NT 972 154
Height gain	1,590 feet (485m)	Ⓑ NT 950 143
Approximate time	4½ hours	Ⓒ NT 934 153
Parking	Roadside parking before Hartside Farm	Ⓓ NT 920 161
		Ⓔ NT 926 164
Route terrain	Remote moorland tracks and rough paths, not always clear	Ⓕ NT 940 167
Dog friendly	Dogs not allowed on access land	Ⓖ NT 959 166
Ordnance Survey maps	Landrangers 80 (Cheviot Hills & Kielder Water) and 81 (Alnwick & Morpeth), Explorer OL16 (The Cheviot Hills)	

One of the attractive features of the Cheviot Hills is their solitude, for the fells show few obvious signs of human intervention and you can often go all day hardly seeing a soul. This walk lives up to that reputation, meandering across the empty moors that encup the Breamish Valley. For much of the way, the paths are faint and do not always correspond to those indicated on the map. Inexperienced walkers are advised to choose a clear day.

🖉 From the lane immediately east of Hartside, take a broad farm track signed to Alnhammoor. After winding over a rise, it falls into the Breamish Valley, crossing the river on a bridge. Climb towards the farm, but approaching barns Ⓐ, leave at a waymark through a gate on the left. Head across the bottom of a field to a second gate, through which turn right on a track.

As it bends behind the farm, keep ahead above the bank of Shank Burn to a ladder-stile. Drop to cross Rowhope Burn and carry on along a grass track. As the valley then curves left, go forward on a trod that initially makes

for Scaud Knowe, a satellite hump on the left of the high ridge of Shill Moor. Climb to a gate at the corner of a fence and through it, then bear left. Continue up the hill, keeping the ground sloping into the valley of Shank Burn on your left. The path is sometimes confused by crossing sheep tracks, but eagle eyes will spot occasional waymarks that guide you roughly south west for the next mile.

As the gradient levels the forward view opens to a vast bowl below Hogdon Law, where Smalehope Burn and Sting Burn have their source before coming together as Shank Burn. The hump of Little Dod eventually appears in view, the path leading you to a waymark just to its right, where there is a crossing path, Salter's Road **B**.

As its name suggests, Salter's Road was part of a salt way, used by traders making for inland markets from the coastal salt pans. In the days before refrigeration, salt was a valuable commodity, necessary for preserving winter meat and fish. The trail was also used by drovers herding stock from the Scottish Highlands for fattening and sale in England. A more secretive traffic lay in the transportation of whisky, illicitly stilled in the higher reaches of these remote valleys.

The way lies to the left of Ritto Hill

Go right, climbing once more over a low saddle before falling to a gate. Beyond, the steadily descending track offers a lovely view along Hope Sike into the higher reaches of the Breamish Valley, a pleasant and perhaps unexpected contrast to the bare moors that rise all around. The track eventually drops to a lane at Low Bleakhope **C**.

A bridleway signed to the right offers a shortcut down the valley back to Alnhammoor. However, the onward route lies left. Keep going as the lane degrades to gravel after High Bleakhope, passing through a stand of timber. Carry on for another ¼ mile to pass another plantation, soon reaching a gate and stile by a waymark **D**. Immediately before it, cut back right

The River Breamish near Hartside

over tussock and climb across the steep bracken-clad slope to a bridle gate. A narrow path continues straight up the hillside, crossing a shooters' track before levelling towards a gate near the top of High Cantle **E**. The lonely moor stretches endlessly away, while to the north is Comb Fell with Hedgehope Hill farther to the right.

Through the gate, the waymarked path branches right to a second gate. Just beyond, watch for the path curving left, initially paralleling the fence but later tending away and rising to a low pile of stones marking the top of Rig

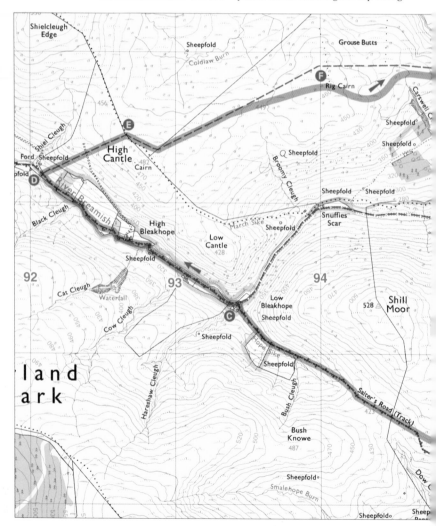

Cairn **F**. The onward route is clear, a serpentine trail across the peaty moor. Those with an eye for detail will realise that it differs from that marked on the OS map, and generally seeks out the easier, drier ground. Eventually crossing a fenceline, stay north of Ritto Hill to a second fence, from which the path descends to a broad gravel track **G** running in front of a large plantation cloaking the deep clough of Linhope Burn. Turn right.

The impressive 60-foot waterfall of Linhope Spout lies only ¼ mile away and can be reached along a permissive path signed off left, a few yards along. The area has a population of red squirrels and, although you might not see them, look out for the remains of chewed pine cones, one of their favourite foods.

The way back, however, continues down beside the trees, subsequently swinging left and right to the cottages at Linhope. Now a lane, it crosses Linhope Burn and leads gently uphill the ¾ mile back to Hartside. ●

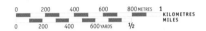

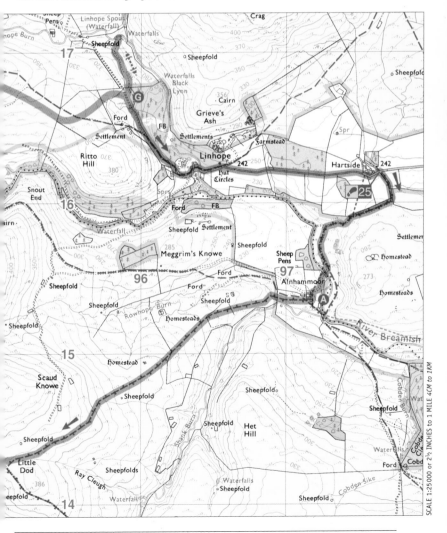

Hadrian's Wall, Housesteads and Sewingshields Crags

		GPS waypoints	
Start	Housesteads Roman fort	✐	NY 793 684
Distance	9 miles (14.5km)	**A**	NY 788 688
Height gain	1,180 feet (360m)	**B**	NY 780 686
Approximate time	4½ hours	**C**	NY 779 706
Parking	Car park at start (Pay and Display)	**D**	NY 790 716
Route terrain	Rugged paths and trackless moorland	**E**	NY 804 726
		F	NY 807 722
		G	NY 810 710
Ordnance Survey maps	Landranger 86 (Haltwhistle & Brampton) or 87 (Hexham & Haltwhistle), Explorer OL43 (Hadrian's Wall)	**H**	NY 811 703

Housesteads Roman fort is one of the best-known features of Hadrian's northern defence and is managed jointly by English Heritage and the National Trust. It sits on the lip of an impressive line of cliffs, overlooking a wild, undulating moss that extends to the north. The route arcs across this untamed landscape, climbing back for an exhilarating finale beside the wall. Inexperienced walkers are advised to choose a clear day.

✐ A path from the car park dips across the line of the vallum and rises to the fort, entry to which is by ticket from the adjacent museum. Continue up beside its western wall to a gate in the top boundary **A** and head away to the left. Many sections of the wall are quite breathtaking, but this must be one of the prettiest, passing beneath a stand of pine crowning the ridge. Breaking from the trees, carry on past a milecastle before dropping off Cuddy's Crags into Ranishaw Gap. Cross a wall at the bottom and turn right over a second stile beside a gate **B**.

Ignoring the broader path, bear right on a trod across rough grazing, signed as the Pennine Way to Leadgate. Crossing a boundary wall, maintain the same course as the way becomes more distinct. Mounting another stile, the path slants down left before resuming its northerly trend, soon crossing Jenkins Burn, which emanates from Broomlee Lough, over to the right. Wind over another shallow rise, shortly meeting a track. Cross diagonally to continue with the Pennine Way doubling left at a waymark a few yards farther on into another dip. Occasional wayposts guide you to a stile in a broken wall and bridge. Keeping the right wall in sight, head up to a stile by a gate in the corner. Cross out onto a

The base of the arched gateway survives at Milecastle 37

track near East Stonefolds **C**.

To the right it passes through a gate into the forest. However, leave the Pennine Way some 100 yds along, branching right on a path marked to Haughtongreen. It meanders across rough ground for ½ mile to an uninhabited cottage. There, keep ahead towards Great Lonbrough and Fenwickhead, the path running briefly beside a wall before swinging left at a waymark. Cross a footbridge and continue between the trees, emerging through a gate at the far forest boundary **D**.

There is no obvious path across the rough moorland of Haughton Common and a compass is necessary in poor visibility. The route lies east of north east, parallel to the outcrop of Crow Crags, picking a way across sometimes boggy tussock. Keep going for a little over a mile until you encounter a faint track **E**. To the right, it winds across Crook Burn and, becoming clear, rises over a low ridge to a gate beside Stell Green **F**.

Walk past the steading and bear right

to join its access track, winding down between Halleypike Lough and Folly Lake. It meanders on for a farther ½ mile, later crossing a bridge beside a ford and joining with another track **G**. Eventually reaching a ruined limekiln, swing left below the wooded bank of Sewingshields Crags.

Climbing to a cottage, the track then bends sharply right **H**. Leave there, picking up the acorn symbols of Hadrian's Wall Path to a gate into Sewingshields Wood over to the right. Pass behind the farm buildings and follow the line of the wall beyond the wood, shortly reaching Milecastle 35. Perched on the edge of the cliff, it enjoys a stunning view; the great hump of The Cheviot breaks the horizon some 30 miles away to the east of north, while 40 miles to the south west lie the northern Lakeland peaks of Skiddaw and Blencathra.

Carry on along the undulating ridge, climbing past a turret to a triangulation pillar marking the high point of the walk. As the line of the wall swings left, there is a view to Broomlee Lough below. Although here only represented by a field wall, the border defence remains a spectacular sight, curving west over King's Hill and Clew Hill. Eventually, after passing through a small belt of wood, Housesteads fort appears ahead, the path dropping to the Roman gateway of Knag Burn at its foot. You can either slip through and follow the outer flank of the wall past the fort back to waypoint **Ⓐ** or work your way around its eastern boundary. In either case, return to the car park along the path from the museum.

The Roman fort, Vercovicium overlooks a gateway beside Knag Burn and slightly post-dates the wall. One of the best-preserved sites along its length, the barrack blocks housed some 800 infantry, overseen by the commandant who had his own residence at the centre of the complex. Perhaps its most famous feature is the latrine block, but there were also storehouses, a hospital and administration buildings. A civilian settlement grew up outside the walls and a bath house has been identified. ●

A strip of pine wood shades the path over Housesteads Crags

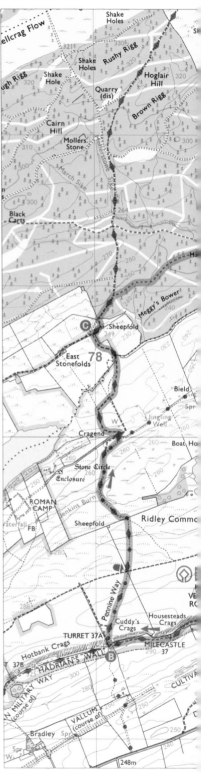

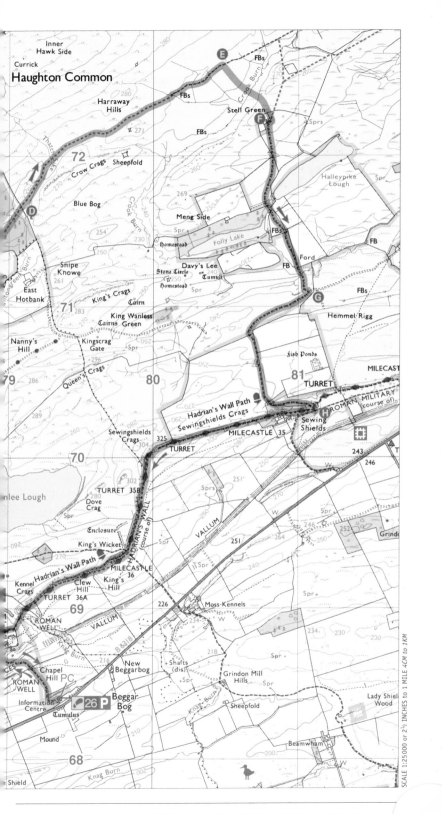

Traquair and Minch Moor

		GPS waypoints
Start	Innerleithen	🖉 NT 335 357
Distance	9¾ miles (15.7km)	Ⓐ NT 330 346
Height gain	1,820 feet (555m)	Ⓑ NT 360 335
Approximate time	5 hours	Ⓒ NT 358 330
Parking	Forestry car park beside B709, ¾ mile south of town (Pay and Display)	Ⓓ NT 368 332
		Ⓔ NT 369 352
		Ⓕ NT 369 345
Route terrain	Good forest tracks and quiet lanes	Ⓖ NT 367 368
Ordnance Survey maps	Landranger 73 (Peebles, Galashiels & Selkirk), Explorer 337 (Peebles & Innerleithen)	

Beginning from the forestry car park, the route follows a minor road to Traquair, there joining the Southern Upland Way along an old track onto Minch Moor. The return is through the extensive forest aproning the northern slopes, where felling has opened spectacular views. The trek ends in an easy stretch above the River Tweed.

🖉 Head left along the B709, swinging right towards Traquair. Walk past the walled estate of Traquair House, eventually reaching the tiny hamlet. Originally a 12th-century royal hunting lodge and forest court, Traquair is said to be the oldest inhabited castle in Scotland. The present building dates from the 15th century when a degree of peace settled on the area. The family remained true to the Scottish throne and following a visit by Bonnie Prince Charlie in 1744, the earl closed the Bar Gates, vowing they would never be reopened until a Stuart was crowned in London.

Go left opposite the war memorial Ⓐ along a climbing lane, signed the Southern Upland Way. Where the lane bends right to Birkenshaw, keep ahead to Minch Moor. Later swinging left towards the sprawling forest, carry on up at the edge of the trees, before long passing a timber bothy set back in a clearing. Walking on, cross a forest road to intercept a second one, higher up.

Take the rightmost of the two paths opposite, rising through taller saplings towards the bare slope of Minch Moor. Eventually breaking from the trees, look to the slopes below, where circular clearings in the heather are an artwork entitled *Point of Resolution* by Charles Poulson. Keep an eye open too for wildlife; buzzard, grouse, curlew and golden plover inhabit the moor, while among those seeking shelter in the trees are siskin and crossbill. Roe deer wander within the forest and in spring you may hear a cuckoo.

Farther along on the right is the Cheese Well, a trickling spring marked with a stone slab. Drovers used to make offerings of cheese to the fairies in return for safe passage, present day travellers leave a coin; ignore the

Looking down from Minch Moor into the Tweed Valley

custom at your peril. Carry on to a signposted junction at the crest of the path **B**.

The summit lies to the right, the path later curving left to the triangulation pillar **C** and the remains of a prehistoric burial. The view from the junction is impressive, but excelled by the all-round panorama from the top, the highest spot in this part of Ettrick Forest.

Return to the signpost and continue

View from the route up Minch Moor

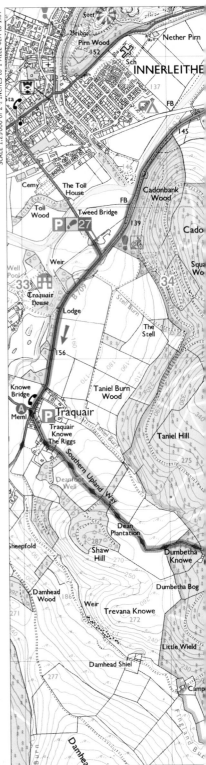

along the Southern Upland Way, which now steadily descends for ½ mile along a forest break. Reaching a junction **D**, there is a grand view into the Lewenshope Valley.

Leaving the Southern Upland Way, take the rough road to the left. After a brief climb it settles into a long descent through the forest below Bold Rig. After 1½ miles, views open into the Bold Burn Valley and the dirt road reaches a junction **E**. Go sharp right, dropping another ¼ mile to a second junction **F**. Now, turn left beside Minchmoor Burn and remain with the main track as it runs along the base of the scenic valley above Bold Burn. On the far side of the Tweed Valley is Cairn Hill, and then, as you leave the trees behind, you can see back over Bold Rig to Minch Moor.

Eventually the track meets a lane **G** at the foresters' hamlet of Glenbenna. Go left and later keep ahead past the junction to Walkerburn. Continue below the steep slopes of Traquair Forest all the way back to the car park. ●

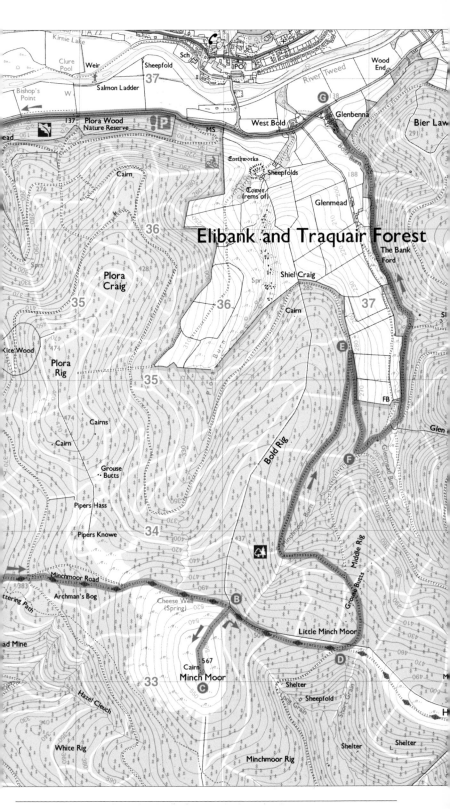

Kirnie Lake

Clure Pool

Weir

Sheepfold

37

Sch

PO

River Tweed

Wood End

Bishop's Point

Salmon Ladder

W

137

Plora Wood Nature Reserve

P

MS

West Bold

G

138

Glenbenna

Bier Law

291

Elibank and Traquair Forest

36

Earthworks

Sheepfolds

Tower (rems of)

Glenmead

188

The Bank

Ford

37

SI

Cairn

276

Plora Craig

428

35

36

Shiel Craig

Cairn

Spr

285

Spr

Kite Wood

474

Plora Rig

Bold Rig

E

FB

270

Glen

Cairns

Cairn

Grouse Butts

Pipers Hass

F

Glenmead Burn

Minchmoor Burn

Pipers Knowe

34

437

Middle Rig

Grouse Butts

Minchmoor Road

Archman's Bog

383

Cheese Well (Spring)

520

B

540

Little Minch Moor

Short Grain

D

White Rig

Hazel Cleuch

Cairn

567

Minch Moor

33

C

550

Shelter

Sheepfold

Shelter

Shelter

Minchmoor Rig

The Cheviot from Harthope Valley

		GPS waypoints
Start	Hawsen Bridge in the Harthope Valley, ½ mile north east of Langleeford	NT 953 225
		A NT 934 229
Distance	13¼ miles (21.3km)	**B** NT 915 233
		C NT 881 222
Height gain	3,280 feet (1,000m)	**D** NT 876 207
Approximate time	7 hours	**E** NT 879 200
Parking	Off road by start	**F** NT 890 198
		G NT 895 193
Route terrain	Remote and rugged moorland paths, strenuous climb to Auchope Cairn	**H** NT 903 194
		J NT 909 205
		K NT 928 218
Dog friendly	Dogs not allowed on access land	
Ordnance Survey maps	Landrangers 74 (Kelso & Coldstream) and 80 (Cheviot Hills & Kielder Water), Explorer OL16 (The Cheviot Hills)	

This ascent of The Cheviot is a challenge demanding fitness and fair weather, yet the anticipation raised by this circuitous approach through a succession of secluded valleys makes it a wonderfully rewarding experience. The most strenuous section is the ascent onto Auchope Cairn, beyond which, a largely paved path relieves the peat expanse of the summit dome. After dropping from Scald Hill, the day fittingly ends in a delightful stroll above Harthope Burn. Less experienced walkers should not attempt this route in poor weather.

Leave the road by Hawsen Bridge, climbing right of a stell or circular sheep pen to find a waypost marking a narrow bridleway that has come up from the lane a little farther back. To the left it rises steadily for ¼ mile through the heather above Hawsen Burn before merging with a broad track. A little farther on, at a waypost, the footpath branches off left, passing another stell on its ascent towards the head of the valley. Higher up, the path converges with another track, but soon after a second waypost, watch for a

crossing path. Go right, left and right again to arrive at a gate in a fence dropping from Broadhope Hill **A**.

The onward path is now clear, gently falling beyond the saddle into the Lambden Valley. In recompense for the relinquishment of your hard-won height, the view along the deepening vale is sublime. Eventually joining a track, pass through a gate and follow it above a small plantation. Binding left, it then passes a second patch of forest. Approaching a dilapidated gate at the far end, swing left to find a path dropping beside the fence. Over a stile, leave the trees and continue along the valley, tacking the bracken slopes. Lower down, cross a couple of stiles before reaching a ford across Lambden Burn **B**.

Climb to the right-most of a pair of gates and follow a trod to Goldscleugh Farm, negotiating another stream to gain its track. Go left through a gate and immediately turn right through a second one. Cross a rough pasture behind the buildings, leaving through a gate at the far end and there go left along a metalled track.

The valley is a pleasant surprise after the bleakness of the high moor. To the left rises the massive bulk of The Cheviot, dramatically rent by the deep clefts of Bellyside and Bizzle burns. Ahead the bare rocks of Dunsdale Crag rear above the burn, which is turned by the protrusion of Fawcett Shank below the foot of Coldburn Hill.

Some 300 yds beyond the forest, watch for a waymarked path cutting left across the moor towards Dunsdale Farm. Join a track up to the house and pass through double gates into a barnyard. Bear right of a corrugated barn, walking through more gates to leave along a rising grass track. Carry on at the upper edge of a plantation

The Cheviot from above Goldscleugh

over the shoulder of Fawcett Shank, bringing the upper College Valley into the scene.

As the track moves away, stay with the fence, shortly reaching a gate in the corner. Continue to a gate opening on the right, through which cross rough ground to a stile. Pick your way left within the boundary of felled forest. Carry on past a rusting hut to a waymark by a gate on the left and bear right to find a clearer trod across the slope above Mounthooly. Over a couple of stiles, keep going among sparse saplings, the way soon turning downhill to pass out through a gate at the bottom. Ford College Burn **C** to reach a broad track.

Follow the track left through a deer gate into the higher reaches of the valley. After some ¾ mile, a waypoint by a stell directs you right. The bridleway heads into a side valley, but after 350 yds, as the path begins to rise, branch off left across the streambed **D**. Passing a large boulder a trod materialises, making for the deep, rocky canyon of Hen Hole. At a second large boulder the way curves right, now aiming for the shallow saddle above and opening a superb view into the ravine. Legend tells that the cascading stream produces a music so sweet as to seduce the unwary to a plunging death in the awesome gape.

Gaining the grassy ridge (where there is a mountain refuge hut a short distance to the right), turn left on a clear path, the Pennine Way **E**. It ascends steeply beside a fence to the impressively rocky top of Auchope Cairn **F**, graced with two monolithic 'stone

men'. *It is the only seriously arduous climb of the circuit,* but is rewarded by one of the finest panoramas in the whole of the Cheviot Hills. Indeed it is claimed that the summits of Lochnagar above Braemar, over 100 miles away to the north west, can be seen.

The onward path is suddenly easy, a well-laid boardwalk, which leads ¼ mile across the morass of peat to a junction of fences and paths **G**. Through a gate and over a stile, a paved path is signed left to Cheviot Summit.

The flags stop short of Cairn Hill, and there is some casting about to find firm footing before you reach the next junction at Scotsman's Cairn **H**.

The path right drops to the head of the Harthope Valley, and serves as an emergency bad-weather escape.

Otherwise, go left again, picking a way beside the fence until the resuming flags once again allow untrammelled passage. After ¾ mile, cross a couple of stiles to reach the triangulation pillar **J**, stranded high on a mound by the

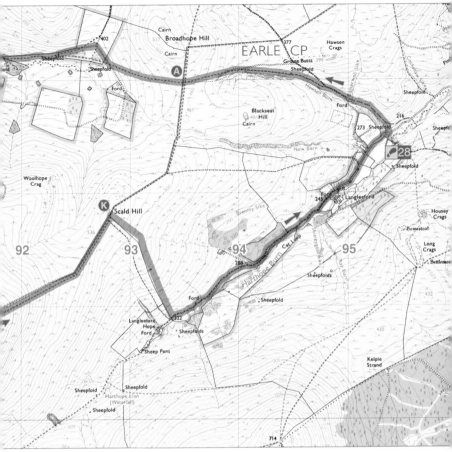

SCALE 1:33333 or 2 INCHES to 1 MILE 3CM to 1KM

erosion of the surrounding peat.

It is a featureless spot with a relatively flat top, but the sense of achievement in reaching the highest point around makes up for the lack of inspiring views. So, having savoured the moment, keep going for another ¼ mile to the end of the flagged path. Over a ladder-stile the ground suddenly falls away, presenting a superb view along the Harthope Valley to the distant sea and islands of Lindisfarne and Farne. Over to the right is Hedgehope Hill, the Cheviot Hills' second summit, while farther on are the distinctive outcrops of Long, Housey and Langlee crags.

Similar to the tors of Dartmoor, they are the stumps of volcanic intrusion, forced through the crust some 380 million years ago.

With the fence now on your left, descend steeply to a shallow col before rising gently onto Scald Hill. After crossing a stile just before the crest Ⓚ, leave the ridge, dropping right. Follow a rough trod beside the fence straight down the flank of the hill, which leads to a track in the base of the valley, just east of Langleeford Hope.

If you have time, it is worth detouring ½ mile back up the valley to see the delightful waterfall of Harthope Linn. The way back, however, is to the left, an undemanding and enjoyable 1½ miles past Langleeford to Hawsen Bridge. ●

Further Information

 ### Safety on the Hills

The hills, mountains and moorlands of Britain, though of modest height compared with those in many other countries, need to be treated with respect. Friendly and inviting in good weather, they can quickly be transformed into wet, misty, windswept and potentially dangerous areas of wilderness in bad weather. Even on an outwardly fine and settled summer day, conditions can rapidly deteriorate at high altitudes and, in winter, even more so.

Therefore it is advisable always to take both warm and waterproof clothing, sufficient nourishing food, a hot drink, first-aid kit, torch and whistle. Wear suitable footwear, such as strong walking boots or shoes that give a good grip over rocky terrain and on slippery slopes. Try to obtain a local weather forecast and bear it in mind before you start. Do not be afraid to abandon your proposed route and return to your starting point in the event of a sudden and unexpected deterioration in the weather. Do not go alone and allow enough time to finish the walk well before nightfall.

Most of the walks described in this book do not venture into remote wilderness areas and will be safe to do, given due care and respect, at any time of year in all but the most unreasonable weather. Indeed, a crisp, fine winter day often provides perfect walking conditions, with firm ground underfoot and a clarity that is not possible to achieve in the other seasons of the year. A few walks, however, are suitable only for reasonably fit and experienced hill walkers able to use a compass and should definitely not be tackled by anyone else during the winter months or in bad weather, especially high winds and mist. These are indicated in the general description that precedes each of the walks.

 ### Walkers and the Law

England
The Countryside and Rights of Way Act (CRoW Act 2000) extends the rights of access previously enjoyed by walkers in

A feral goat, wandering on the flanks of Black Braes

England and Wales. Implementation of these rights began on 19 September 2004. The Act amends existing legislation and for the first time provides access on foot to certain types of land – defined as mountain, moor, heath, down and registered common land.

Rights of Way

These are either 'footpaths' (for walkers only) or 'bridleways' (for walkers, riders on horseback and pedal cyclists). A third category called 'Byways open to all traffic' (BOATs), is used by motorised vehicles as well as those using non-mechanised transport. Mainly they are green lanes, farm and estate roads, although occasionally they will be found crossing mountainous areas.

Rights of way are marked on Ordnance Survey maps. Look for the green broken lines on the Explorer maps, or the red dashed lines on Landranger maps. They give a right of passage over what for the most part, is private land. Deviation from the line, other than in areas designated as access land, can be regarded as trespass.

Local authorities have a legal obligation to ensure that rights of way are kept clear and free of obstruction, and are signposted where they leave metalled roads

Access Land

Under the Countryside and Rights of Way Act (CroW 2000), certain types of open land: mountain, moor, heath, down and registered common land have been designated access land, where you can leave the path and wander on foot at will. Access Land is indicated on current Ordnance Survey Explorer maps by a light yellow tint surrounded by a pale orange border. Orange-coloured 'i' symbols show the location of permanent access information boards.

Restrictions

Landowners can legally restrict access to such land for short periods. There may also be a requirement to keep dogs on leads and dogs may be banned from certain moors. However, these restrictions do not apply to rights of way crossing the land.

General Obstructions

Obstructions can sometimes cause problems, for example, overhanging vegetation, wire fences, locked gates or cattle feeders. In most cases, it will be possible to negotiate the obstruction without causing damage, but should it be necessary to remove the obstruction, remove as little as necessary to secure passage. A common difficulty occurs when the path across a ploughed field has not been reinstated. Although it might seem more sensible to walk around the field edge rather than trample a crop, this is actually a trespass. There is a long-standing view that it is permissible to deviate should the defined line become impassable. However, this cannot be wholly relied upon and if in doubt, retreat and report the problem to the local authority.

More detailed information can be obtained at www.naturalengland.org.uk

Scotland

Walkers in Scotland have long enjoyed a moral and de facto right of access, now enshrined in *The Land Reform (Scotland) Act 2003*. This carries with it responsibilities, which are outlined in the Scottish Outdoor Access Code. The three key principles are:

- Respect the interests of other people
- Care for the Environment
- Take responsibility for your own actions

The following common situations affect walkers.
- Farm steadings - There is no legal right of access to farm steadings but in practice many existing routes go through them.
- Fields - Keep to paths where possible or walk around the margins of a field under crops.
- Fences, dykes and hedges - When crossing walls, dykes, fences and hedges use a gate or a stile where possible, otherwise climb over carefully to avoid damage.
- Golf Courses - You have a right of access

to cross golf courses but must avoid damage to the playing surface and never step on to the greens. Cross as quickly as possible, considering the rights of the players.

- Deer Stalking - During the hunting season check to ensure that the walks you are planning avoid stalking operations.

More detailed information can be obtained at www.outdooraccess-scotland.com.

 ## Useful Organisations

Association for the Protection of Rural Scotland
Gladstone's Land, 3rd floor,
483 Lawnmarket, Edinburgh EH1 2NT
Tel. 00131 225 7012
www.ruralscotland.org

Campaign to Protect Rural England
128 Southwark Street, London SE1 0SW
Tel. 020 7981 2800
www.cpre.org.uk

Camping and Caravanning Club
Greenfields House, Westwood Way,
Coventry CV4 8JH
Tel. 0845 130 7633
www.campingandcaravanningclub.co.uk

Forestry Commission
Silvan House, 231 Corstorphine Road,
Edinburgh EH14 5NE
Tel. 0845 3673787
www.forestry.gov.uk

Historic Scotland
Longmore House, Salisbury Place,
Edinburgh EH9 1SH
Tel. 0131 668 8600
www.historic-scotland.gov.uk

The National Trust
Membership and general enquiries
PO Box 39, Warrington WE5 7WD
Tel. 0844 800 1895
www.nationaltrust.org.uk

The National Trust for Scotland
Wemyss House, 28 Charlotte Square,
Edinburgh EH2 4ET
Tel. 0844 493 2100
www.nts.org.uk

Northumberland National Park Authority
Eastburn, South Park, Hexham NE46 1BS
Tel. 01434 611675
www.northumberland-national-park.org.uk

National Park Visitor Centres
Ingram Tel. 01665 578890
Once Brewed Tel. 01434 344396
Rothbury Tel. 01669 620 887

Northumbrian Water
Leaplish Waterside Park
www.nwl.co.uk/Planyourbreak.aspx

Ordnance Survey
Romsey Road, Southampton SO16 4GU
Tel. 08456 050 505
www.ordnancesurvey.co.uk

Public Transport
Traveline
Tel. 0871 2002233
www.traveline.org.uk

Ramblers' Association
2nd Floor, Camelford House,
87-90 Albert Embankment,
London SE1 7TW
Tel. 020 7339 8500
www.ramblers.org.uk

Ramblers' Association Scotland
Kingfisher House,
Auld Mart Business Park,
Milnathort, Kinross
KY13 9DA
Tel. 01577 861 222
www.ramblers.org.uk/scotland

Scottish Natural Heritage
Silvan House, 3rd Floor East,
231 Corstorphine Road,
Edinburgh EH12 7AT
Tel: 0131 316 2600
www.snh.org.uk

Scottish Rights of Way and Access Society
24 Annandale Street, Edinburgh EH7 4AN
Tel. 0131 558 1222
www.scotways.com

Youth Hostels Association
Trevalyan House, Dimple Road, Matlock,
Derbyshire DE4 3YH
Tel. 01629 592700
www.yha.org.uk

Scottish Youth Hostels Association
7 Glebe Crescent, Stirling FK8 2JA
Tel. 01786 891 400
www.syha.org.uk

Tourist information

North East England
Tel. 0844 249 5090
www.visitnortheastengland.com

Tourist information centres
Alnwick: **01665 511333**
Amble: **01665 712313**
Bellingham: **01434 220616**
Berwick-upon-Tweed: 01289 330733
Corbridge: 01434 632815
Craster: 01665 576007
Haltwhistle: 01434 322 002
Hexham: 01434 652 220
Morpeth: 01670 500 700
Once Brewed: 01434 344 396
Rothbury: 01669620887
Seahouses: 01665 720 884
Wooler: 01668 282 123

VisitScotland
Head Office, Ocean Point 1, 94 Ocean
Drive, Leith, Edinburgh EH6 6JH
Tel. 0845 2255 121
www.visitscotland.com

Tourist information centres
Eyemouth: 01890 750678
Hawick: 01450 373993
Jedburgh: 01835 863170
Kelso: 01537 228055
Melrose: 01896 822283
Peebles: 01721 723159
Selkirk: 01750 20054

Weather forecasts;
Weathercall - Met Office forecast by phone
(Durham, Northumberland, Tyne & Wear)
Tel. 09068 500 418
(Fife, Lothian and Borders)
Tel: 09068 500 422
www.weathercall.co.uk

 ## Ordnance Survey maps for Northumberland, & the Scottish Borders

The area is covered by Ordnance Survey
1:50 000 scale (1 ¼ inches to 1 mile or 2cm
to 1km) Landranger sheets 67, 73, 74, 75,
79, 80, 81, 86, 87 and 88. These all-purpose
maps are packed with information to help
you explore the area. Viewpoints, picnic
sites, places of interest, caravan and
camping sites are shown, as well as public
rights of way information such as footpaths
and bridleways.

To examine this area in more detail, and
especially if you are planning walks,
Ordnance Survey Explorer maps at
1:25 000 (2 ½ inches to 1 mile or 4cm to
1km) scale are ideal:

OL16	(The Cheviot Hills),
OL42	(Kielder Water & Forest)
OL43	(Hadrian's Wall)

Explorer 307	(Consett & Derwent Reservoir)
Explorer 332	(Alnwick & Amble)
Explorer 337	(Peebles & Innerleithen)
Explorer 338	(Galashiels, Selkirk & Melrose)
Explorer 339	(Kelso, Coldstream & Lower Tweed Valley)
Explorer 340	(Holy Island & Bamburgh)
Explorer 346	(Berwick-upon-Tweed)

To get to Northumberland use the Ordnance
Survey OS Travel Map-Route Great Britain
at 1:625 000 scale (1 inch to 10 miles or
4cm to 25km) or Road Map 3 (Southern
Scotland & Northumberland) at 1: 250 000
scale (1 inch to 4 miles or 1cm to 2.5km).

Ordnance Survey maps and guides are
available from most booksellers, stationers
and newsagents.

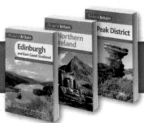